# NETAJI BOSE
Father of Secularism

# NETAJI BOSE
## Father of Secularism

Prof. V Anto

an imprint of Highlyy Publishing LLP

ISBN: 978-93-6009-544-4 (Hardback)
First Published : 2024
Copyright © Author

*Publisher's Note:*

All Rights reserved under International Copyright Conventions. No part of this publication may be reproduced, stored in a retrieval system, or transmitted in any form or by any means, electronic, mechanical, photocopying, recording or otherwise without the prior written consent of the publisher and the copyright owner.

The content of this book is the sole expression and opinion of its author(s), and not of the publisher. The publisher in no manner is liable for any opinion or views expressed by the author(s). While best efforts have been made in preparing the book, the publisher makes no representations or warranties of any kind and assumes no liabilities of any kind with respect to the accuracy or completeness of the content and specifically disclaims any implied warranties of merchantability or fitness of use of a particular purpose.

The publisher believes that the contents of this book do not violate any existing copyright/intellectual property of others in any manner whatsoever. However, in case any source has not been duly attributed; the publisher may be notified in writing for necessary action.

> Cataloging in Publication Data--DK
>
> Courtesy: D.K. Agencies (P) Ltd. <docinfo@dkagencies.com>
>
> Anto, V., 1966- author.
>
> Nethaji Bose : father of secularism / Prof. V Anto.
>
> pages cm
>
> ISBN 9789360095444 (hardback)
>
> 1. Bose, Subhas Chandra, 1897-1945. 2. Nationalists--India--Biography. 3. Statesmen--India--Biography. 4. Indian National Army--History. 5. India--History, Military--20th century. 6. India--Politics and government--1919-1947. I. Title.
>
> LCC DS481.B6A58 2024 | DDC 954.035092    23

Published by :

# HOW
ACADEM/CS

an imprint of Highlyy Publishing LLP

Correspondence Address :

4/30 A II Floor, Double Storey Buildings
Vijay Nagar, Delhi-110009
Editorial: +91 9811026449
Sales : +91 9999953412
Email: info@howacademics.com
Website: www.howacademics.com

# Contents

| | | |
|---|---|---|
| | *Preface* | *vii* |
| | *About the Author Prof. Anto* | *ix* |
| 1. | Our Childhood Hero | 1 |
| 2. | Total Freedom | 5 |
| 3. | The Great Escape | 9 |
| 4. | The German Story | 13 |
| 5. | Submarine Voyage – An Epic Journey | 17 |
| 6. | The Japanese Story | 21 |
| 7. | INA – a miracle of History | 25 |
| 8. | Conquest of Andman Islands | 29 |
| 9. | The Burma Campaign | 33 |
| 10. | Flag Hoisting at Moirang | 41 |
| 11. | The Battle of Imphal | 45 |
| 12. | The battle of Kohima | 49 |
| 13. | Retreat to Singapore | 51 |
| 14. | Atomic Bombs and Surrender | 55 |
| 15. | Asylum in Russia | 59 |
| 16. | The Red Fort Trials | 67 |
| 17. | The Naval Mutiny 1946 | 71 |
| 18. | Freedom with Partition | 75 |

| 19. | An Ungrateful Nation | 83 |
| 20. | The INA.......A Tamil Army? | 93 |
| 21. | Netaji Bose - Father of Sacrifice | 99 |
|  | *Index* | *103* |

# Preface

A book on Netaji always causes a buzz for the simple reason that Indians anywhere in the world can never forget this superman of our freedom struggle. Whether it's a child, a teenager, youth or elder; the love for our Netaji endures forever. Whenever the word Netaji Bose is spoken, the first question asked is about his alleged plane crash. Almost 80 years after that purpoted accident, Indians refuse to believe he actually died in that fateful crash. There is incredulity and disbelief that the prince charming of our freedom struggle could actually go with a whimper after making the mighty British empire cringe during his INA march through the jungles of Malaya and Burma. There is also anger that after 8 decades that there is not a shred of light on his actual death and the whereabouts of his dead body. Everybody on this planet has a birthday and a death day. However it is only the chosen few who refuse to have a death remembrance day. One such noble soul is our Netaji Bose. So much information of Bose has been buried from our school and college text books simply because of the central government policies by first PM Nehru and then by his daughter PM Indira Gandhi. All our popular freedom heroes including Gandhi, Nehru and Patel have a resting place for their dead bodies, called in Hindi as a Samadhi. However Netaji alone does not have a Samadhi. Successive central governments under Atal Behari Vajpayee and V P Singh did try to dig into the secret of Netaji Bose's death but nothing came of it. Even the present central government under Mr. Modi has not been able to get an epitaph on Bose for the last one decade of his PM rule.

This book aims to fill that void and dis-information campaign against Netaji Bose. This book intends to set the record straight on our Prince of Patriots who brought freedom to our door-step. This book will burn a hole in the conscience of all politicians who have simply made empty talk on how they consider Bose as the ultimate freedom hero of India. This book is the answer to all those critics who have made false allegations against this first son of India, who gave his everything for the freedom of our motherland. This book will smash the myth that it was Ahimsa that brought freedom for India, when the Quit India Movement fizzled out under Gandhi and it was the Red Fort Trials that brought ultimate independence to India. Generations would scarcely believe that this brilliant ICS officer from Bengal would put an end to the mighty British empire, setting their sun in various countries of Asia and Africa in quick succession, immediately after the freedom of India in 1947. The submarine voyage of Bose is the stuff legends are made of you can't get tougher than that. The Great Escape from India to Europe was actually a Leap of Faith by Bose as a last ditch effort to save his health from the grimy British jails of India and Burma, so that he could to bring independence to his mother-land.

Last but not the least, this book will set to rest speculation on the actual death of Netaji Bose since the authentication has been given by our MP, Dr.Subramaniam Swamy himself in an open press conference a few years ago. No one has dared to question his surmise on the death of Bose in a freezing Siberian prison after spending many years in total anonymity there, inspite of the best efforts of the press and public of India to discover his whereabouts. Inspite of vested interests trying to sell the aircraft theory, documentary evidences have clearly proved no such crash ever happened in Taiwan on the faterful day of 18th August, 1945. This book will serve as the final epitaph for this true son of India, who gave his blood, sweat and tears for the liberation of our motherland. No more will there be any tall stories of Bose living in India in disguise, dressed as a swami ji or living in deep jungles as a hermit having relinquished wordly pleasures. All these cowardly and false depictions of Bose after his disappearance from public life in 1945, will be put to rest. This then is the final book on Netaji Bose's Death Theory and will be the clarion call for all Indians to unite together and build a monument for him in Delhi, Calcutta and Madurai as a final resting place for his immortal soul. There is absolutely no more need to fight over whether the copper urn at the Renkoji temple in Tokyo actually contains Bose's ashes or not. More important to realize is that our Netaji is dead and he needs to be given a memorial befitting a true hero and the first son of India.

# About the Author
## Prof. Anto

Right from his childhood days, Prof. Anto had a deep fascination for the freedom struggle of India, particularly, the important role of the Indian National Army and its leader, Shri Netaji Subash Chandra Bose. As a young school kid his interest in Netaji Bose grew deeper especially since he found there was very little literature on him in his school text books. In fact, he even questioned his class teacher on why so much importance was being given to Gandhi but very little importance was being given to Bose. During his college days at Loyola College (Madras) he used to spend long hours in the college library researching the role of Bose in the freedom struggle. He used to pour over the Encyclopedia Brittania which in those days was an authority on world history. One must remember there was no computer or google in those days. His research led to the study of the country of Burma, which had sheltered Bose during his sojourn in south-east Asia. He took a deep fascination for Burmese history and culture. His interest in the freedom struggle led him to due further research on the second world war. He found that most of the history books narrated only the victories of the British and Americans, while ignoring the feats of the German and Japanese armies. His war research further took him to the wars of the Indian army after independence, one of the wars that fascinated him was the China War of 1962. He found very little literature on the China War since it had been deliberately played down by the Congress government in the center. One of the books that fascinated and inspired him was the Himalayan Blunder written by former army officer, Brig. John Dalvi, who had personally taken part in the tragic war. It was then that he realized how terribly PM Nehru had misjudged the situation and led India to humiliation. What infuriarated him was the way Nehru refused to accept his blunder on the China policy and how he witch-hunted the officers of the Indian army taken prisoner by the Chinese.

Prof. Anto has a deep fascination for nature and is a tree grower in his native city of Coimbatore in southern India. He is a lover of animals and birds and hence he has dedicated his home in Coimbatore to the conservation of wild birds that visit his 50-odd trees. There are close to 25 species of birds that enter his home forest every day along with around 3 families of squirrels. He also feeds the dogs around his home, who also visit his home forest. He has a deep love for our national game, Hockey, which he promotes in all schools and colleges of his native Coimbatore district. He runs hockey training programs in various schools of Coimbatore, developing young talent.

His passion for the INA took a wonderful turn when he stumbled upon the Netha Ji Subash Chandra Bose Memorial National Welfare Foundation in Chennai. Situated in the locality of Ayanavaram, this NGO was operated by Capt. Dasan, a former Tokyo cadet of the INA. Both Prof. Anto and Capt. Dasan developed an excellent relationship centred around the principles of Netaji Bose. Capt. Dasan used to recollect his golden days with the INA very often to Prof. Anto. He used to mention how when he was still a very young boy in his late teenage, he joined the INA as a raw recruit in Malaya, where his family had already settled down from India. Capt. Dasan, who hailed from a poor, Plantation labour Tamil family from Malaya, was almost immediately selected to be training art of the 40 Tokyo Cadets to be sent from south-east Asia to Japan for intensive training in various military domains. All these cadets were sent to the Imperial Military College in Tokyo for training in various disciplines of physical warfare. Capt. Dasan was trained as a pilot for the air force. Unfortunately during the end of their military training in Tokyo, the atom bombs were dropped on Hiroshima and Nagasaki, which led to the ultimate surrender of Japan to the allied forces. The cadets were disbanded and taken prisoner by the landing American troops who promptly dispatched them back to India as POWs.

After our independence in 1947, the formation of AIR India from the erstwhile Tata Airlines, opened up vacancies for commercial pilots. Since there was a shortage of pilots, Capt. Dasan was immediately absorbed as an airline pilot given his experience of training as a Pilot as a Tokyo Cadet. Capt. Dasan had a long and distinguished career in AIR India as a senior pilot and flight commander of commercial operations. He has flown to various countries and has also ferried Prime Minister Nehru and his cabinet colleagues on a number of occasions. One of the brightest spots in his flying career was when he was called upon to fly transport aircraft during the 1962 China War. He has often recounted those tragic days, when as a pilot high in the sky, he had a birds eye view of the battle field across the eastern Himalayas in Arunachal Pradesh. His eyes used to turn moist as he recalls the mayhem created by the Chinese army as they smashed across the MacMahon line to decimate the Indian army, which was simply outnumbered and outgunned. He remembers flying food, clothing and supplying sorties over the besieged town of Tezpur as they prepared to take the thrust of the invading Chinese army. He remembers how everything went topsy turvy for the Indian Government as it strained to function under the artillery attack of the Chinese army.

Capt Dasan specifically felt that if only the Indian Air Force had been properly pressed into action, the Indian army would not have taken the kind of beating that they did from China. His opinion was based on the fact that China did not operate a single aircraft as they attacked us across the Himalayas in Arunachal Pradesh or in Ladakh. The reasons were simple. China did not have a proper operational air base in Tibet and hence had to rely on aircraft all the way from mainland China, a distance of at least a thousand miles. The intelligence failure of the Indian Government led to this important aspect of our defence preparedness being underlooked. When Indian air bases were so close to the Himalayas, we failed to use our fighter and bomber aircraft with due diligence. Many military experts from India and abroad have come to the general consensus that the lack usage of our fighter and bomber aircraft cost us the war. In fact, the air chief was specifically quoted to have said in a press conference that there was no role for the Indian air force fighter and bomber aircraft in the 1962 war. Some experts have hinted at a total lack of co-ordination between the Indian Air Force and Indian Army Chiefs during those trying days of 1962. Added to that was the fact that our defence minister of those times, Mr. Krishna Menon, had absolutely no clue on how to tackle China, both diplomatically and militarily.

One of the outstanding achievements of our Netaji Chennai foundation was to pressurize the Tamil Nadu state government during the centennial birth anniversary year in 1997 to install a life size statue of Shri Netaji Bose at the famous Marina Beach of Chennai. The Marina Beach is a landmark beach in Chennai city (formerly Madras city) noted for its particularly long coast line. It also boasted the life size statuses of some of the most prominent personalities of Tamil culture and history, on the famous shore roadl leading upto the famous Mahatma Gandhi Round Tana. When we approached Shri Kurunanidhi, who was a Chief Minister during that period, we were told to wait, since there was strong opposition to installing the statue of any North Indian leader in Tamil Nadu. However we continued to meet the CM's son, Mr. Stalin, who personally intervened and inspite of opposition from the Congress MLAs in the assembly, was able to install the Netaji statue on the marina beach. Today the statue of Netaji Bose is truly an unforgettable monument on the marine drive of Chennai city, being an inspirational piece of architechture to remind the future generations of the sacrificial spirit of our freedom fighters of a bygone era. This is the statue that we continue to garland and pay our homage to for the last 25 years, especially on January 23 which is Netaji Bose birthday. Needless to say the Thevar community of Chennai and Madurai had a large part to play in influenzing the government decision. We must continue to remember that without this community's support, the INA would not have performed so heroically during the Burma operations against the British army. Their youth stood like a rock against the onslaught of the British army in the jungles of Burma and the hills of Manipur and Nagaland.

Capt. Dasan and his NGO used to hold regular meetings on a monthly basis which included old INA veterans, members of society, teachers, retired government officers, etc, among others, who had genuine interest on the life and times of Netaji Bose and the INA. This NGO was also in close touch with many former INA veterans including Capt. Laxmi, Capt. Yadav and others. The INA veterans from Tamil Nadu, particularly the Madurai region, also used to attend these meetings. They were also in close touch with Dr. Anita Bose, the daughter of Netaji Bose, residing in Germany. On at least 2 occassions we were blessed by her visits to India from Germany, once in 1996 and again in 2000. During the second visit in the year 2000, one particular incident rankled above the others. The Chief Minister of Tamil Nadu at that time, Mr. Karunanidhi, had been invited for a felicitation of Dr. Anita Bose at a five-star hotel in Chennai. Since he was the CM and he was politically aligned to the Congress Party in the centre, he declined to come for fear of aggravating the Sonia Gandhi family. However to appease the powerful Thevar community in his political party alliance, he decided to send his son, Mr. Stalin for the occasion. But even that did not materialize since his son declined the invitation in the last minute. For lack of time, the organizers contacted Tamil cine actor Mr. Sharath Kumar and his wife Radhika, who were kind enough to fill up the void. It was really tragic that Mr. Karunanidhi was not savvy enough to honour the daughter of Netaji Bose, whose INA consisted of many people of Tamil origin. It was truly an unkind cut and brought back bad memories.

One of the most prominent guests to our NGO was Capt. Laxmi. In the year 2001, she was invited as the chief guest to Velammaal School at Moggappair in Chennai. The school management was run by the Thevar community, a community famous for its martial background. This was the very same community from which Mr. Pon Muthu Ramalingam hailed, the famous person who did a remarkable job recruiting army cadets for the INA from the rural areas of the Tamil regions around the historic city of Madurai. The school management had installed a bust of Netaji Bose and wanted capt. Laxmi to inaugurate the same in the school premises. Prof. Anto was deputed by the Bose foundation to escort Capt. Laxmi to the school venue. He travelled in the school car to the ancestral Chennai home of capt. Laxmi in the heart of the city at Harrington road. Prof. Anto was thrilled to visit the vicinity of his school, the Madras Christian College Higher Secondary School which brought back fond memories of his early youth.

Capt. Laxmi took an instant liking for prof. Anto, who at that time was in his mid-thirties. Prof. Anto also took a liking for this rather tough old lady who was in her late 80s. Having read so much of INA literature during his childhood itself, he knew he was in the company of an extra-ordinary woman, a medical doctor by profession who had sacrificed her blooming medical career in Singapore just to serve the INA. Prof. Anto was also acutely aware that the Jhansi Rani Regiment of the INA had created a world record for India by being the only all-women fighting military unit operating in the second world war. No other western country like America, Germany or England fielded a fighting women's military unit, teaching the world a lesson on women emancipation. He found it unbelievable that he was sitting in a car, right next to the women's brigade commander, who had physically trekked through the jungles of Malaya and Burma to reach the Manipur border in 1944. Looking at this bespectacled yet tough old lady, Prof. Anto felt a pang of remorse that this daring lady had not been properly felicitated by the Indian Government, either by PM Nehru or Indira Gandhi. While it was true that Nehru hated the guts of Netaji Bose, he should have treated this brave lady with more respect and caring. When he could offer a central cabinet minister post to Gen. Shah Nawaz Khan in the early 1950s, what stopped him from offering a similar post to capt. Laxmi. Being a medical doctor, Nehru could have offered her the post of union Minister for Health.

At this point, its pertinent to remember that capt. Laxmi was the only competitor to Dr. Abdul Kalam when he stood for elections to the post of the president of India. Dr. Kalam was the unanimous choice of the Congress, but since the ruling BJP government under Shri Atal Behari Vajpayee were happy with him as the Missile Man of India, they also backed Kalam for the President's post. The Communist Party of India (CPI) decided to field Capt. Laxmi as their presidential candidate. It appeared a lop-sided contest since the Congress-BJP combine were at a numerical advantage. Yet capt. Laxmi gamely contested and lost to Dr. Kalam however in hindsight, Dr. Kalam should have allowed capt. Laxmi to have contested all alone since she was a freedom fighter and there should have been basic respect given to such rare people. While Dr Kalam was by himself an excellent candidate, due priority should have been given to a former freedom fighter like capt. Laxmi. While Dr. Kalam was an excellent scientist, a prominent Freedom Fighter would always be given more weightage in any civilized society. However all the political parties did not make an issue of this and hence capt. Laxmi had to single handedly stand on the CPI ticket against the combined might of the BJP and the Congress parties, putting up a united presidential candidate for the first time after many decades. The reason also appeared pretty obvious. The Congress Party did not want to antagonize Dr Kalam, since he would be a stumbling block to them if they came back to power in the 2004 national elections to follow. Moreover they certainly did not want to support capt. Laxmi, since she was the favourite disciple of Bose, who was a sworn enemy of the Congress. All in all, Dr Kalam was sworn in as the President of India with a thumping majority and capt. Laxmi went into oblivion.

Little was I to know that within leass than 3 years, capt. Laxmi would stand for the Presidential Elections 2003. Accompanying capt. Laxmi, he felt happy to be sitting next to an old lady, who not many decades ago had put the fear of God in the British troops fighting in Burma. Capt. Lasmi's team of fully armed lady soldiers also pitched in to help as medical staff to the injured INA soldiers and officers. In fact, capt. Laxmi was holding twin responsibility in the INA firstly, as the Brigade commander of the Jhansi Rani Regiment and secondly, as the commander of the Medical Corps across the battle front. The conversation in the car veered around to my family and it soon became obvious that capt. Laxmi's grand nephew happened to be my old college mate in Loyola College, Madras. His name was Nikhil Swaminathan and he also studied with me in a Chennai primary school, although he left very early. Capt. Laxmi was eager to meet my wife and kids. The fact that both of us were actually Malayalees originally from kerala also helped cement our bonds. She explained that her family migrated from a village called Annakkara in Palakkad district of kerala to Madras city even before she was born. Being from the neighbouring Trichur district of kerala, I was trying to figure out if I had ever crossed Anakkara village.

We reached the school well on time and was accorded a grand reception. The chairman of the Velammal Group of Instituitions was there to recieive us, having come all the way from Madurai to Madras just to meet capt. Laxmi. we were told that the entire family of the hosts were die hard admirers of Netaji Bose. Moreover, as already mentioned, they belonged to that particular community called the Thevars that was known for its immense participation in the Burma campaign of the INA. Hence they had specially invited capt. Laxmi, whom they felt carried the flame of Netaji Bose on her shoulders. We had tea with the chairman and the school Principal along with the staff members. Then we were taken around the school campus which was quite impressive. Finally, we were accorded a grand reception on a Red Carpet laid out in the school playground. I led capt. Laxmi to the edge of the red carpet, waiting for the opportune moment to walk along with her for the red carpet welcome.

Suddenly the band struck and capt. Laxmi threw off my protective hand holding on to her wrist for her support. For a moment I wondered what had happened but once she started marching to the beat of the band, there was no stopping her. Its then I realized how much the spirit of the INA was still in her bones. She marched like a champion, giving least regard to the fact she was nearing ninety in age. I trundled behind her, feeling like a worm following a tigress. The entire crowd of students, teachers and parents stood mesmerized at the splendid display of parade marching. She took the stage and gave us a wonderful speech on her days in the INA. One sentence of her speech would never, ever leave my memory she specifically mentioned that if Netaji Bose had been present today he would certainly have enjoyed the admiration that the entire crowd had for the old INA. We left the school after a rousing send-off by the management.

Later that evening I was invited to meet capt. Laxmi in her home at Harrington Road in Chennai, very close to my old school. Capt. Laxmi was thrilled to meet my wife and blessed both my son and daughter. It was probably the best blessings they ever received come as it did from one of the most famous daughters of our freedom struggle. The photograph of that meeting is still preserved in out home and would rank as a priceless gift that one receives once in a lifetime. We had dinner with capt. Laxmi and got to meet her extended family of brothers and sisters. It was a few years later that I got to know she was competing against Dr. Abdul Kalam for the post of the President of India. Unfortunately the arithmetic in the Parliament was not enough for her to win the elections and Dr. Kalam emerged the winner. Of course, India did get a wonderful president in Dr. Kalam, but we certainly missed a military freedom fighter to lead us. What surprised me was that even a die hard admirer of Netaji Bose like PM Atal Behari Vajpayee did not push for Capt Laxmi, knowing very well that at 90 years of age, this would probably be the last election she would be contesting. It is my personal view that for that 2003 presidential election that BJP government could very well have rallied behind capt. Laxmi and probably supported Dr. Kalam to stand for the 2008 elections.

# 1. Our Childhood Hero

As a school boy of 10 years, we remember reading an article of the freedom struggle in our history text book. It mentioned a very small paragraph of Netaji Bose and his INA. The same chapter had many paragraphs on Gandhi ji and the Congress party. Six years later an English film was launched by the Indian Government called GANDHI. Since my family was going to watch this tax-free movie which also won some Oscar awards, we had the opportunity of watching an English man play the role of Gandhi. This was really terrible, since noted Bollywood maestro Nasruddin Shah was supposed to play this role. What was even more shocking was that there was no character called Netaji Subash Chandra Bose in that entire movie. Imagine if Laxman was missing in the epic Ramayana, would it be a complete story?

From that day on, our only quest was to find out why such a famous freedom fighter was being treated in such a cavalier fashion by the political establishment. We have been on the trail of Netaji Bose and his INA for the last 40 years and the kind of research results we have experienced has been nothing short of astonishing. It has become abundantly clear that the prime candidate to become India's first Prime Minister was Netaji Subash Chandra Bose. The kind of lies that were bandied about his career and activities by the Congress Party officers were mind boggling. The systematic way in which Character Assassination was done on him, after his dissapearance from civilization in August 1945 is something the whole of India should be ashamed of. After our independence in 1947, the first PM Jawaharlal Nehru took special interest in spreading more rumours and lies about Netaji Bose. Nehru simply hated the guts of Bose, just because he personally regarded him as his greatest threat to becoming independent India's first PM.

The famous story of how Bose had returned to India after independence in the disguise of a Hindu Monk was propogated by the Congress Party, just to hide the truth that Netaji Bose was killed in a Russian prison in freezing Siberia under the leadership of dictator Joseph Stalin in the early 1950s. The rumours were so cheap and malicious, making digs on his impeccable personal life. This was obviously a mass, concerted effort by Nehru and his cohorts to make sure the fair name of Bose was sullied forever. This trend continued even after Nehru's death, when his daughter Indira Gandhi became PM. But both Nehru and Indra were very clever in giving a public image of showing respect to Netaji and his legendary INA. While Nehru inducted INA veteran, Col.Shah Nawaz Khan into his cabinet soon after independence, he refused to allow any INA soldier to join the Indian Army, either as an officer or sepoy. This was done to prevent any mutiny in the army at any future point of time. However this cost the Indian Army dearly during the Kashmir War of 1948 against Pakistan, when we were short of war experienced troops. The officers and sepoys of the INA were battle hardened troops in the jungles of Malaya and Burma, whose vast experience would have helped the Indian army immeasurably. Pakistan, on the other hand, welcomed their INA veterans into their regular army, which helped them become victorious in certain sectors of the Kashmir war. General Mohammed Kiani and Col. Habib Ur Rehman provided excellent service to Pakistan during the Kashmir war of 1948. Both of them had distinguished service in the INA jungle operations in Burma, which proved to be decisive in the long run.

One of our personal experiences with Netaji's chosen officers were during our old Madras days when we were the ambassador of the Netaji Bose National Welfare Foundation under Capt. Dasan, one of the 40 Tokyo Cadets hand-picked by Netaji Bose during the Burma campaign. Capt. Dasan had trained in Tokyo as an INA cadet in the Japanese Imperial Military Academy. Among the 40 chosen cadets, he was nominated for training as a pilot officer. Unfortunately before this group could complete their military graduation, Japan surrendered to the Americans in August 1945. Hence the Tokyo Cadets were disbanded and had to flee Japan back to their homes in South East Asia. Capt. Dasan finally made it back to India and became a commercial pilot for AIR India, then owned by the TATA group. Capt. Dasan rose up to become the chief commander of the airline and one of the missions he remembers was during the 1962 war with China. Flying transport aircraft during this tragic war, he was witness from high in the sky, to the total break down of our infrastructure against the Chinese Army. He was morally shattered at the mess the political leadership under PM Nehru exhibited against the Chinese government.

The more we researched Netaji Bose the more we got to know of his magnani-mous nature to both his friends and enemies alike. Actually Bose had the greatest admiration to Gandhi ji, to whom he was the one to give the title "Father of the Nation" which was announced through one of his public radio broadcasts in Radio Japan. Bose also was extremely civil to Nehru, whom he considered his colleague in the Congress party. However history has recorded with ample evidence how disdainfully Nehru treated the Indian National Army volunteers and soldiers during his interaction with them after the dissapperance of Bose in august 1945. Till Bose was in India, Nehru pretended to confide in him. Once Bose left India for good in 1941, Nehru worked overtime to sabotage all the efforts of Bose for India's freedom. There is no doubt that concerning his relationship with Bose, Nehru was at once selfish and jealous of a person whose charisma far outstripped his own in front of the public masses. Nehru truly believed that he would be India's first Prime Minister and that the only person who would contest that seat would be Subash Bose. Hence Nehru had a raging jealousy for Bose who was far more intellectual than he could ever hope to be, as well as Bose's mass adulation among the people of India. Moreover Nehru had an inferiority complex about his educational background against Bose, since he was painfully aware that Bose was the only ICS officer of the Congress Party during the freedom struggle. There were many advocates and barristers in the Congress Party but Bose was the only civil servant who had the guts to quit his job in the ICS just to join the freedom struggle. Today Netaji Bose's story is what legends are made of. There is no historical equalent in the entire freedom struggle of India against the British, except possibly the legacy of Tippu Sulthan.

## 2. Total Freedom

The concept of Total Freedom was espoused by Netaji when he wanted the British to quit India in the early 1930s. However, Gandhi was emphatic that British leave India in a phased manner and that too on a non-violent mode. This was the main reason that his call for Quit India came only in 1942, almost one full decade after Bose had already given his clarion call to the Congress party. Bose had early on realized the folly of Gandhi ji's Non-Violent Struggle against the British as one in which freedom would take a long time to come after numerous negotitations on both sides. Bose wanted the British to quit India immediately unlike Gandhi who wanted them to leave in a phased manner after handing over Dominion Status to us.

The start of the second world war in 1939 opened up a huge opportunity for India to grab freedom from the British, but Gandhi ji's policy of supporting the western allies against Adolf Hitler proved to be a damp squib. Britian badly needed Indian soldiers to fight for them against the German and Japanese armies in Europe, Africa and Asia. Without loyal and sub-servient Indian soldiers, it was impossible for the British army to conduct the war around the globe. Instead of seizing this golden opportunity to turn the entire Indian population against the British rule in India, Gandhi ji made the Himalayan blunder of supporting the British against fascist Germany. By doing so, Gandhi inadvertently allowed time for the British to divide the Indian population on religious lines. By allowing the British off the hook, Gandhi even requested more and more Indian soldiers to join the war against Germany and Japan. The irony of the whole matter was that Indian soldiers of the British Army in Burma were actually killing the INA soldiers under Netaji Bose fighting alongside the Japanese army. However this aspect of Indians killing their own people was kept a secret from the Indian population due to a News Blackout introduced by the British during the second world war. Had this news reached the local public, there would most certainly have been a mass outcry and internal agitation against the British in India.

Finally, it was only during the Red Fort Trials of 1946, that the entire India burnt in flames when news of INA officers being given the Death Sentence became local public news. This led to massive public protests and demonstrations that forced even Nehru to come out of his shell and offer his legal support to the convicted INA officers, after Gandhi specifically ordered the entire Congress Party to stand behind Netaji's Indian National Army war trials at the Red Fort. The mass demonstrations spread to the Royal British Navy at both Bombay and Karachi harbours, where Indian sailors opened fire on their British officers. Many of the Naval ships docked at Bombay and Karachi harbours were captured by these sailors and their British officers arrested internally. The entire country ground to a standstill and the world watched while Britain fumbed against the native Indians, angered over the INA concocted trials. The British had no option but to call off the trials and all the INA officers were exonerated of their crimes.

However the actual outcome of the 1946 Naval Mutiny was that the British finally decided to exit India immediately. It is true that after the start of the second world war in 1939, Gandhi had lost the steam of his Non-Violent ahimsaa struggle. The Congress Party had split into 2 parts due to the religious divide of hatred which the British had infused into India. One part of the Congress under Gandhi maintained secular outlooks. The other part simply became the Muslim League under Mohammed Ali Jinnah, who wanted a separate Muslim homeland for all Muslims of India. Using the second world war as a screen, Gandhi launched the Quit India Movement in 1942, which did not take off in a big way. For the next three years till the end of the war in 1945, there was absolutely no political activity by the Congress party. It had became a dead and decadent party simply following the course of the second world war. The British meanwhile promised Gandhi that they would most certainly grant "dominion status" to India, once the war was over. But nothing happened even after and Japan surrendered to USA and the war came to an end in August 1945. For close to one year the Congress Party did absolutely nothing to continue the freedom struggle.

Then came along the Red Fort Trials in 1946 and the entire country leapt in up in flames, angered that the INA officers were going to the gallows. This triggered the patriotic sailors in the Royal British Navy to go revolt against their commanding officers. Historians are very clear on the fact that if the Naval Mutiny of 1946 had not happened, the British would certainly not have quit India in 1947. Gandhi's Non-Cooperation Movement had the wind knocked out of its sails the moment he decided to support the British army against

Germany in 1940. It was indeed a deep stroke of fortune that the Red Fort Trials became a catalyst for the a mass movement to happen in 1946. Historians have rightly said that the Congress Party rode piggy-back on the INA soldiers to gain ultimate independence for India, without giving any credit for Netaji Bose and his INA for having instigated this mass movement. It is cruel twist of history that a man who gave his life blood for India's freedom was not there to savour the independence in 1947. It is correctly said that it's the curse of the nation which ignored its true freedom heroes, that makes poverty and corruption such an open issue for the last 75 years of independence. As the old adage goes, A Nation that Ignores its Real Heroes will continue the Suffer The Curse of Ingratitude.

# 3. The Great Escape

With realization having dawned for Bose that it was now worthless to stay in India under the leadership of Gandhi, he decided to make a clean break out of India in January 1941. He had a choice of leaving northwards across the Himalays, eastwards across Burma, northwest across Afghanistan or take the sea crossing to the middle east across the Arabian sea. Crossing the Himalayas into Tibet was very dangerous given the high mountain passes and cold weather. Eastwards was also risky since he had to cross the entire stretch of Burma which was totally under the control of the British. The sea route across the Arabian sea would be fraught with great risks since getting the right ship or large boat without close contacts was near impossible. Hence he opted for the softest option, crossing Peshawar in the North West Frontier Province into Afghanistan. His first mission was to first leave his home unnoticed by the British secret police who were monitoring him continuously. This is where we see Bose as the master of disguise. He cleverly uses the dress of a Muslim visitor to his home to exit without arousing suspicion. He is driven by his own nephew from Calcutta city to a remote village in Bihar where he boards a train to Peshawar via Delhi. From Peshawar he treks across the Durand line to enter Afghanistan, an independent country even in those days. His immediate mission was to meet the Italian embassy staff in Kabul and get their protection.

However there is an inordinate delay in entering the embassy and the danger to Bose deepens since Kabul happened to be the hub for all secret agents from various countries jockeying for power in central Asia. There were secret police of Britain, Russia, Germany and a host of other nations hanging around the capital city of Afghanistan. Moreover Netaji was staying in disguise at the home of some Indians settled in Kabul. He was an outsider there and the local police were suspicious of his presence. It was truly fortunate that the Italian consulate, under orders from Mussolini, made haste and prepared a fake passport for Bose showing him as an Italian citizen. With this passport, Bose was able to travel through neighbouring Uzbekistan and finally reach Germany to meet with Adolf Hitler.

Historians marvel at the raw guts of Subash Bose, a mass leader of a populous country like India, who could travel over 2000 kms over land at high risk of being discovered by the omnipresent British police present everywhere. Being 6 foot tall and having a familiar bald head over a chubby, bespectacled face, Bose's looks were unforgettable to any Indian citizen and the British Raj in those days of the freedom struggle of the 1930s and 1940s. Yet he defied all logic and threw caution to the winds, when he embarked on such a death-defying world expedition, all for the sake of attaining freedom for his mother land. It was such a crazy move that Bose made, knowing very well the chance of success was extremely slim given the huge distances he had to travel and the number of hostile countries that he would have to traverse across. There were British and American secret agents floating all around Asia, who were all armed and given prior information to take Bose captive, dead or alive. Even in Afghanistan, there were Russian and Afghani spies who were there to accost him at the slightest suspicion. Bose simply followed the old maxim fortune favours the brave !!

From Afghanistan, Bose crossed into Soviet central Asia, and via Uzbekistan, takes a long land route in the north western direction. Although these regions were desolate and far from the prying eyes of the western powers, there was the presence of the Soviet secret police everywhere. After months, Bose reached Moscow, still retaining his disguise as an Italian citizen Mr. Count Orlando Mazzotta. He arrived at the Italian embassy in Moscow and after a few days there, he was flown to Rome to meet the head of the Italian government, dictator Benito Mussolini. The meeting with Mussolini went off well and upon Bose's express request he was flown to Berlin to meet the fuhrer, Mr. Adolf Hitler.

The meeting with Hitler is something that has been explained in many different ways and the photograph of his hand-shake with the dictator is now legendary. There have been critical reviews on why Bose would shake hands with the someone who ordered the mass genocide of Jews across Europe. But the truth is that in early 1943, the world was only beginning to glimpse the atrocities that Hitler was wrecking on the Jews of Europe. Bose had no inkling to the enormity of Hitler's destruction of the Jewish community of Europe. The meeting went off very well and Hitler was impressed by the intellectual prowess and acumen of Netaji bose. As per Bose's request he was allowed to travel to Japan to meet Mr. Hedikki Tojo, the dictator of Japan. Since Bose could not be flown across Europe, he was given a German Navy submarine to reach South East Asia where the Japanese army had already conquered large territories.

From there it was a matter of time before he squared the deal with the Japanese high command to resuscitate the dormant INA in South East Asia. His brilliant idea of using the POW Indian soldiers as new recruits of the INA paid off very well, as these experienced war veterans were able to guide the totally fresh recruits with due deligience. The INA turned out to be a huge success mainly due to the guts of these volunteers who were ready to sacrifice everything for the freedom of our nation. The INA volunteers were deeply shaken by the amount of risks that Bose took to leave India for South East Asia, through Europe. They realized that their leader was no ordinary Indian. A man who could travel half way around the world braving extreme risks, even though he came from a rich family, definitely meant that the person was extraordinary and truly daring. The British had obviously under-estimated their intended quarry while he was in India and now paid the price of not properly patrolling him, night and day. However, the end result was that Bose broke through the security cordon around him to make good his escape to Europe.

## 4. The German Story

Bose's entry into Germany was not without its drama. As a coloured man from Asia, it was almost impossible to visit Nazi Germany, except on special invitation of the government under Adolf Hitler. Bose was given permission only because he was one of the chief enemies of the British government, who wanted him dead or alive. Since Hitler hated the British, he found a common voice in Bose. However, even after allowing Bose entry into his country, Hitler was in no hurry to meet him. Hitler was still gathering acute information on Bose before meeting him. Plus, the time was not ripe, even though Bose was looking for an early appointment.

Meanwhile Bose devoted his time to meeting the Indian repatriates and exiles in Germany. He started the Indian Legion, an armed brigade comprising of Indian soldiers of the British army who had been captured by the German army during the recent wars in Europe and Africa. These Indian POWs were promised freedom from jail if they joined the Legion. These activities were encouraged by the German High Command since it helped build up anti-British feelings in Germany. The Legion troops reported directly the Wehrmacht, or regular German Army. Later they came under control of the notorious SS Troops, reporting directly to Hitler himself.

One of the biggest admirers of Indian soldiers under the British army was none other than one of the most brilliant military strategists the world has ever seen. Field Marshal Erwin Rommel of Germany, popularly known as the Desert Fox, had very good regards on the fighting capabilities of the Indian troops working in the British Army, especially in the African theater of the Second world war. As commander of the Afrika Korps of the German Army, Rommel continuously came under attack of the Fourth Indian Division under the British 8th Army. Being an extremely brilliant yet humane military officer, Rommel had to use all his field tactics to avoid getting hit by the Indian troops. Military historians have always maintained that Field Marshal Rommel was the actual winner of the African theatre of the Second World War. Pitted against numerically superior and well-supplied British and American forces, Rommel won many battles in Africa, even though he lost the final war there. Even in final defeat, Rommel executed such amazing manoevres in the desert using his tank warfare capabilities to maximum capacity. In many instances, impending defeat was converted to victory, by his brilliant command of his loyal troops. During the final stages of the tank battles in the North African western desert, Rommel took a pounding from the Fourth Indian Division of the British 8th Army, which led to his final defeat. While Rommel exited to Germany, he ordered his subordinate officer to do the actual surrender formalities only with an Indian Officer of the Fourth Indian Division. Even in victory, the British were humiliated, since Rommel maintained his stance that it was the talented Indian soldiers who had defeated his German army and not the white British officers.

It is a perfect irony in history that the very same Indian soldiers of the Fourth Indian Division worked under the German Army one year later in 1943. After the African desert operations in 1942, many of the captured POWs of the German Army were recruited by Netaji Bose to join the Indian Legion in Europe. During that period they worked directly under the German Army command. By a bizarre turn of events, Field Marshal Erwin Rommel addressed the Legion and remembered with admiration the guts and determination with which the Indian troops had fought against his tank forces in North Africa. He later on met Netaji Bose in Berlin just before the latter embarked on his submarine voyage to Asia and complimented him on the courage of the Fourth Indian Division troops in North Africa.

The meeting with the German chancellor, Adolf Hitler, was the icing on the cake. Even though it was a long delayed meeting, it was finally arranged at the insistence of his Gestapo, or secret police. The under-cover agents of the Gestapo had various inputs on Bose and most of it was pointing to a man of real substance. Hence they made sure that Hitler did catch up with Bose. During the meeting while Hitler was probing Bose, the latter was very focused and actually demanded that Germany give him maximum military support to take on the British from outside Indian territory. Hitler had already chalked a plan with his military generals that made the Indian revolutionary forces join ranks with the Japanese army in Asia. Since India was on the conquest map of the advancing Japanese armies, it would only be better for Japan to directly help the Indian resistance fighters in Asia, than for the German army to back up the Indian resistance forces. Hence Hitler decided to charter a submarine to carry Bose to South East Asia from Europe, since ferrying Bose by aircraft across Europe would be too risky, given the second world war scenario.

During his stay in Germany during 1942, Bose was the toast of the large Indian community diaspora of Berlin. He was invited to almost all programs that featured talks on nascent freedom struggles going on in Asia and Africa against the British empire. As a senior leader of the Indian freedom struggle, he was seen as an icon against imperialism. His wide intellect and gracious manners made him a big hit in all social gatherings. His mastery of the German language also helped him make good friends among the German public. The fact that Hitler had openly announced that Indians also belonged to the Aryan race, made Bose more attractive to the German populace. His tall stature and bespectacled face had an aura that few Germans could resist. Also the speeches of Bose were a big hit in Germany, since he spoke of armed revolution in contrast to the non-violence movement of Gandhi. Bose used every opportunity he got to take up the cause of Indian independence and garner support from every corner of Germany.

# 5. Submarine Voyage – An Epic Journey

Every successful military commander in the world has had to face the litmus test in his life- the life turning decision which is fraught with high personal risk and danger. Bose had to take a call when Hitler was kind enough to sanction a submarine to carry him underwater from Europe to Asia, since it was decided it would be too dangerous for him to attempt an air passage through some of the most militarized flight routes in the world. A submarine voyage would be much slower and would have its owns risks since the subs in those days had just been tested a few years ago.

On February 08, 1943, the German U-boat numbered U-180 set sail from the harbour of Kiel in Northern Germany with the entire crew and two foreign visitors. Till the submarine actually took off, none of the crew were aware who the 2 foreign guests were and the destination of the vessel. As the submarine dived into the North Sea, it set sail for Norway and then veered off around Britain to set a course due south for Africa. The visitors were introduced by her Captain to the crew as Mr. Bose, a freedom fighter from India and his camp aide, Mr. Abid Hassan.

This was the first time that both these illustrious Indians were travelling in a submarine. Moreover this was not a routine short trip of a few days, but a marathon journey under-sea for over one month. It was unlikely the submarine would come to the surface during this journey due to the risk of detection by enemy troops. Both the visitors managed to ride out their initial bout of sea sickness. The naval crew were amazed at the calmness of both the visitors whenever the sea got rough and there was inclement weather outside. In fact, the visitors never complained on anything even though they were VIP guests of Hitler himself.

In his memoirs written many years after the end of the second world war, the commander of this submarine, Capt. Werner, had described Subash Bose as an extremely well mannered foreigner and an extreme intellectual. During the course of their long voyage from Europe to Africa, the commander did get into long conversations with Bose, since the latter was adept with the German language. Capt. Werner found Bose to be a warm person with strong family ties back in India. Bose was also well versed in military strategy including Naval warfare. It was then that his companion, Abid Hassan, explained to an astonished Capt. Werner that Bose had stood all-India fourth rank in the ICS exams held every year under the British Raj. He enjoyed the company of his Indian visitor, who spent most of his waking hours reading books, playing chess or having deep political and strategic discussions with his companion.

There were a few occasions for anxiety during the submarine voyage. One was when they were detected mid-sea by American aircraft flying over the open sea. The U-Boat had to dive into the sea, even as the enemy brought in bomber aircraft to drop depth-charges into the sea. Fortunately the submarine escaped damage due to the rich experience of her captain, who was a shrewd mariner. Another time, the sea turned choppy and the U-Boat was tossed and turned around in the rough waters and strong under-currents. The skipper rode out the storm assisted by her battle hardened crew. Bose and Hassan also endured the storm with determined grit. There were brighter moments too when the U-boat sunk two enemy ships along the way. It was a rare feeling to be inside a submarine, when a kill was being planned or executed.

The German sub now planned to transfer Bose and Hassan to a Japanese sub which was supposed to meet them off the eastern coast of Africa. Around 45 days of voyage, the German sub was able to set up the rendezvous point off the coast of the island of Madagascar in the Indian Ocean. The Japanese sub was headed by an experienced Veteran Mariner, who had orders to pick up a senior Indian leader on the high seas. The transfer was effected mid-sea using a rubber dinghy which left the German sub even as the sea was extremely rough. Capt. Werner gave the choice to Bose if he wanted to wait for the sea to become calm before effecting the transfer. As a seasoned military analyst Bose knew that every minute both the submarines were floating on the sea was a ticking time bomb. If any enemy aircraft spotted them, both the subs would be attacked immediately and there would be no time to submerge. Bose knew that this was the best opportunity he would get to reach Asia and any delay would prove costly in the long run. So inspite of the German crew warning the 2 visitors against leaving the sub immediately, Bose decided to take the Leap of Faith. Inspite of the rough sea, Bose made a break for the Japanese sub floating a good 100 metres away. He and capt. Abid were thoroughly wet when they boarded the Japanese sub and ware welcomed aboard. Later on, he came to know from both the German and Japanese crews that most of the German and Japanese crew members had assumed that the rubber dinghy would sink in the choppy waters. It was indeed a miracle that Bose and Hassan lived to tell another day.

This secret submarine voyage of Netaji Bose is rated by many historians as a turning point in the Second World War and also India's war for independence against the British. Here was a mass leader of the Indian public who had the raw guts to flee his own country, forge an alliance with a totally new country and then have the audacity to travel close to 2500 kms under the sea, just to attain freedom for his motherland. Here was an extremely educated intellectual who was equally adept at physical hardships, who would go to any extent to secure his country's independence from an imperial power. Here was a patriot who had the guts to seek an appointment with one of the cruelest dictators of the world and then convince him to lend him a full scale naval submarine to carry him across three continents. Here was a civilian who had the raw guts to undertake a 90 day voyage across two huge oceans, including a mid-sea dinghy boat ride in extremely rough, shark infested waters. This same man had the temerity to travel by land across Northern India to cross over to an extremely semi civilized country called Aghanistan, where the local Pathans carried with them loaded rifles just like ordinary sticks. This man further crossed over from Afghansitan to hostile Soviet union territory with an Italian passport wangled from the Italian embassy in Kabul. He visited Moscow and was diplomatically escorted from there by flight to faraway Rome, before he finally met Adolf Hitler in Berlin.

# 6. The Japanese Story

After entering the Japanese submarine off the coast of Madagascar near eastern Africa, Bose travelled further up the Indian Ocean to reach the port of Sabang, in the island of Sumatra, now part of Indonesia, formerly called the East Indies. Upon arrival, Bose was given a ceremonial welcome by the occupying Japanese military station befitting a head of state. Later, he was taken around the island and then airlifted to Singapore, which had fallen into Japanese hands a year before. Singapore was converted into the head of the South East Asian operations of the Japanese Army, since it was so strategically located between the Pacific Ocean and the Indian Ocean zones of naval conflict against the British and American forces.

In Singapore, Netaji was introduced to the top military commanders of the Japanese Army and also the Naval officers. Here too, Bose was given a ceremonial reception and it was very obvious that all the local Japanese officers had been ordered to give utmost respect to Bose, befitting a head of state. After a few days, Bose was flown to Tokyo to meet General Tojo, head of the Japanese Imperial forces, who was the de facto president of Japan. Tojo had deep regards for Bose, having studied his entire background including his stay in Germany. While initially there was slow pace of progress between Bose and the Japanese army, the speed picked up once Tojo realized he was dealing with a strategic genius. Bose interacted extensively with the resident Indian community in Tokyo and thus built up a strong rapport with the diaspora. He was invited for social gatherings and functions all across Tokyo and was the toast of the town. The Japanese public actually began to like him once they heard his passionate speeches on his plans for the liberation of India. The Japanese already had warm feelings for India since many of them still practiced Buddhism and its founder Buddha was born in India. There was also a rumour going around in Japan, that Bose was possibly the incarnate of Buddha and the liberator of enslaved India.

With time ticking away, Bose was introduced to Rash Behari Bose, the original founder of the INA and a very patriotic Indian living in Japan spearheading the freedom struggle from Tokyo. Behari realized that Bose was indeed the ideal person to take the freedom struggle forward from Japan, since he himself was unable to physically handle all the pressure. He realized that Netaji Bose had a unique personality that was very pleasing to the Japanese. Rash had done a great deal in keeping the flame of independence alive among the Indian diaspora in Japan. He had become quite elderly and now realized that Subash Bose had the fountain of youth in him that made him a natural successor to him. Rash willingly requested the Japanese government and the military junta to transfer the entire control of the INA to Netaji Bose. The Japanese wasted no time in transferring Bose to Singapore where the operational plans for the entire conquest of South East Asia were already under way.

Bose reached Singapore by special aircraft from Tokyo. He wasted no more time and immediately got the INA up and running. The first thing he did was to get Capt. Mohan Singh, a captured POW of the British Indian army, to organize the rank and file of the INA. Capt. Singh was an energetic officer but was highly reactive due to which he had several rub-ins with the Japanese army command. At one point of time he was placed under house arrest and Bose was made the supreme commander of the INA.

The INA raising day was assigned on 21st October 1943 at the Esplanade grounds in central Singapore. More than 60,000 troops paraded in front of their supreme commander. The day was marked by a fiery and patriotic speech by Netaji Bose that brought tears to the eyes of the local onlookers. Marked by his world famous rhetoric "Give me blood and I shall give you freedom", the speech transformed the hearts of many bystanders including Dr. Laxmi Swaminathan, who had come searching for a medical practitioner job in Singapore. Dr. Laxmi had graduated from the famous Madras Medical College and as a young doctor she was keen to work in Singapore among the local Tamil population there. Just by chance, she attended the public INA meeting and was immediately mesmerized by the speech of Netaji Bose, which kindled the patriotic fervor in her.

Hailing from a socially active family in Chennai and having a famous mother in the name of Mrs. Ammu Swaminathan, Dr. Laxmi had very active genes in her blood. Her parents originally belonged to the town of Aanakkara in the Palakkad region of the then erstwhile Madras Presidency, they had all migrated to the capital city of Madras, a thriving port city on the eastern coast of India and the fourth largest city of the British Raj in India. Dr. Laxmi was a bright medical school graduate and had a promising and lucrative career in front of her in Singapore, a remote British colony in South East Asia. Yet she decided that she wanted to join the medical corps of the INA, knowing that Netaji Bose represented the last but pragmatic route to ultimate independence for India.

Dr. Laxmi took an instant liking for the supreme commander of the INA, Shri Netaji Bose. She found him to be direct and to the point. No beating around the bush like some of the older Congress Party leaders of those times. Comparing Bose with Gandhi, she realized why Bose was fondly referred to as the Netaji.....he was certainly a born leader, blessed not only with excellent oratorical skills but also a fast executioner of plans. On his part, commander Bose found Dr. Laxmi a natural lady officer, what with her immaculate manners and fine family upbringing. Bose immediately decided that Dr. Laxmi would not only head his military medical team but would also be the commander of the first Lady's Regiment, which he named the Rani Jhansi Regiment.

And thus was born the first Ladies Army Regiment of the second world war. No other country during WW2 had a separate all-ladies regiment, not even the highly developed armies of Germany, USA, Japan, UK, Russia or Italy had an all-women military unit. Women in military uniform normally represented medical staff like doctors or nurses. India set the world record in the second world war for having close to one thousand lady troops in uniform, most of them infantry soldiers with intense weapon training. Even the accompanying Japanese army were surprised at such a large consignmemnt of Lady troops in the INA. These troops distinguished themselves during the Burma campaign with their valour and resilience in Jungle warfare. Some of the lady troops doubled as staff nurses and medical orderlies during the war operations to take care of the wounded INA soldiers. Here the medical experience of Dr. Laxmi came to the fore as she rallied the lady staff around her, building a core team of nurses and orderlies. Bose was so taken up by the doughtiness and loyalty of the Jhansi Rani Regiment, that he decided to join them by road ,during the retreat back from the Indian border to Singapore, even though he had the option of being air dropped by a Japanese plane back to Singapore.

# 7. INA – a miracle of History

There is no doubt that the INA was well and truly India's National Army. Drawn up from volunteers from all over India and abroad, it was the biggest Voluntary Natonal Army during the second world war. The INA was indeed a mini-India with Indians from all corners of the country and abroad enlisting into its rank and file. There is a mis-conception that the INA was a north Indian army. But in reality it was a mixed army with maximum representation from the Tamil people due to two main reasons. One reason was that since the INA was established in South East Asia, the large Indian population living on the plantations in Malaya and Burma were more than willing to enlist their youth after hearing the passionate speeches of Bose. The second reason was the presence of a dynamic local leader of southern Tamil Nadu (then called Madras Presidency) called Pon Muthu Ramalinga Devar or Devar-iyya. Hailing from the militant community of Thevars in the Madurai region, Mr. Devar was a strong supporter of Netaji Bose during the freedom struggle. When Bose left India for Germany, he continued to have close contact with him with overseas contacts. Using his excellent contacts and position of respect in his large community in both India, Burma, Malaya and Singapore, Devar motivated the Tamil youth to join the INA in all capacities. His clarion call encouraged many men and women youth to join the INA in large numbers. Hence in reality, the INA was actually a Tamil dominated army.

The mother of the INA was the Indian Government-In-Exile under the leadership of Netaji Bose operating from Singapore. This was only the second Government in exile operating during the second world war. The first was the French exile government operating from London, after France was overrun by Germany during the second world war in 1940. Charles de Gaul was the head of that exile government who went on to become the President of France at the end of war. Unfortunately, Bose could not emulate him, although he was the most worthy leader of that time to don the mantle of the first Prime Minister of independent India. Fate snatched him away from civilization 2 years before ultimate freedom came.

The Indian Government in exile or simply called GIE, was truly a phenomenon in South East Asia during the world war times. The GIE had its own flag, currency and bank, its own postage stamps and of course its own Army, the INA. Netaji Bose as its supreme commander and head of the provincial government had diplomatic relations with 13 countries, including Croatia, Italy, Japan and Germany among other nations. Upon the formation of the GIE and the INA on October 21, 1943, the first move was the declaration on war on both Britain and USA.

The INA was close to 60,000 troops, including the back-up, reserve troops stationed in southern Burma (now called Myanmar) and Siam (now called Thailand). It was truly a multi-cultural organization filled with patriotic Indians from all over India and south-east Asia. The outstanding feature of this army was that it was purely Voluntary Force with no salary paid. Only food and accommodation was provided that too depending on the conditions. During the course of the war in Burma and Malaya, half the INA perished due to a combination of food and medical shortage. Many lost their lives to injury and blood loss with shortage of basic medicines including pain killers and Penicillin. Many lost their life to tropical diseases including Malaria and Dysentery. Many suffered due to snake bite and leech attacks. Many suffered from vitamin deficiencies and retarted bone and organ growth. Many were raw volunteers, including young women, who were handling weapons and fire arms for the first time. Inspite of all these short comings, the INA troops were a first class fighting force. During the various battles in the jungles of Malaya and Burma, the INA distinguished itself in battle, taking on the might of the British imperial army, which was fully funded from the British Raj in India. There were many commendations for the INA troops from battle hardened Japanese army officers and also grudging admiration from enemy British army officers.

The British government tried to down play the role of the INA, by giving it the moniker "Japanese Inspired Force or simply JIF. The British wartime Prime Minister, Winston Churchill, had ridiculed the INA as a " rag, tag and bob outfit masquerading as a national army". His words were proven wrong when the INA attained ultimate independence for India by stirring up mass, patriotic fervor leading to riots against the Red Fort Trials in 1946. The following year the British quit India fearing for their lives. Even in retreat and ultimate defeat, the INA was able to influenze public opinion and turn the tide for freedom. Such was the patriotic wave created by the INA on the psyche of the common Indian citizen.

Netaji Bose divided the INA into major Brigades. He named them after the leaders of the Congress Party leading the freedom struggle in India. He named the brigades as Gandhi, Nehru, Patel and Subash brigades. Such was his magnanimity towards Gandhi that inspite of their major differences of opinon, he continued to call Gandhi Father of the Nation, a title he first made popular when he broadcast freedom messages from Radio Japan and Radio Berlin. Bose went a step further by giving a brigade name to Nehru, who always had mistrust and jealousy for Bose. It was really sad that the rivalry between Nehru and Bose was largely a one sided affair, where Nehru pretended to be in step with Bose but all the time he was worried about the mass popularity of Bose. Nehru was extremely jealous of Bose in that he was an intellectual who could also physically lead the masses, without the mask of being an ahimsa proponent. Also Nehru very much knew the only person who could be his competitor to being the first Prime Minister of India was Netaji Bose alone. Hence he was desperate to pally up to Gandhi, while making sure that Bose was isolated in the ahimsa group. On his part, Bose did not harbour any ill-will to Nehru, treating him very respectfully as a party colleague but knowing fully well that he wanted to become the first PM of India at any cost. Bose did not have the cheap mind-set of Nehru to bite behind the back of party colleagues. He was too much of a gentleman for such dirty politics.

It's very important to remember that there was no SALARY paid to the troops of the INA, since it was purely a voluntary army. Unlike all the other armies that participated in the second world war like Russia, Britain, America, Japan and Italy, the INA did not pay a single penny in cash to its soldiers or officers. This is truly one of the most surprising aspects of the second world war, where Indians all over south and south-east Asia flocked to join a purely volunteer army just on the foundations of patriotism and national pride. Those Indians from south-east Asia trekked all the way by land from either Malaya, Singapore or Burma to join the INA recruiting centers. Volunteers from India had to take the boat ferry from south India to Burma. Some took the ferry form Calcutta to Rangoon or Chittagong, whichever was closer or practical to them. From these port cities they had to trek it overland to reach the recruitment centers of the INA. The soldiers were provided only food,clothing and accommodation. Many had joined without informing their families in fear of being stopped from travelling either by the British authorities in India or by their own family members. Many lost their way travelling into Burma and Malaya, often retracing their paths till they reached their final destination.

Unknown to many Indian citizens ,the INA special task force was even air dropped into Indian territory by the Japanese army and navy. Some of the undercover agents of the INA was slipped into Indian waters by the Japanese naval ships and submaries from the Arakan coast of Burma and later from the Andaman Islands after its capture by Japanese navy. Some were para-dropped into eastern and southern coast of India but were shot down due to the cunning intelligence activity of the British army spies. Many were captured alive by being betrayed by their contacts in India who were trapped by the police in India. Many lost their lives during the sea travel on boats and rafts in the middle of the night, to avoid detection by the British navy patrolling Indian waters in the Bay of Bengal. Some of the agents who opted to parachute into Indian coasts along Madras, Visakapatnam, Orissa and the entire Bengal coast (including modern Bangladesh today) landed on very hostile territory, including marshes, thick & thorny jungles, swampls, etc. Some paratroopers got their parachutes entangled in branches of large trees managed to extricate themselves and reach terra firma. Others were not so lucky and could not disentangle themselves before daylight and were easily detected by British patrols early in the morning. Many were taken prisoner, some were shot at sight by trigger happy British soldiers.

# 8. Conquest of Andman Islands

One of the biggest morale boosters and indeed a major victory for Netaji Bose's Government-in-exile was the conquest of the Andman Islands. The significance of this conquest was not lost on the British government since the Andaman & Nicobar Islands represented the police state of the off-shore British empire in India. These remote group of Islands in the Indian Ocean represented the ugly face of the British Raj in India, since the biggest and most notorious mass prison for political detainees was here. Called the Cellular Prison in English and Kaalaa Paanee in Hindi, this prison used to sound the death knell of all political prisoners in mainland India. Torture was very common in this huge prison. Only hard core political activists were bundled off from the Indian mainland to the Andaman Islands to serve life terms and sometimes summary executions. It was almost impossible for a political prisoner in India consigned to the Cellular Jail to ever return back home alive. Hence the word Kaalaa Paanee which literally meant in Hindi as "black water" signifying death.

Hence it was with a sense of grim satisfaction that Bose landed on December 30th 1943 at Ross Island, the seat of the British governor, administering the Andaman & Nicobar Islands. Escorted by a commodore rank Japanese Naval officer, Netaji first brought down the British Union Jack and then unfurled the Indian Tricolour on the giant flag staff in front of the Governor's office. He immediately left for Kaalaa Paanee prison, where a contingent of left over Indian political prisoners, awaited his triumphant entry. Anticipating the arrival of the Japanese Navy, the British administration had emptied out the prison and carried most of the sensitive prisoners with them back to the Indian mainland, while spot executing many other "dangerous" convicts. All important files and documents were carried away by them back to India, while the rest of the office files were simply burnt down. Fortunately the British did not burn down their buildings and other civil infrastructure on the Islands, due to shortage of time. The arrival of Netaji Bose in the Andaman Islands was more symbolic than a major territorial victory for the INA. His arrival heralded to the world that

India was capable of regaining her lost territories from the British empire, using military might and not some fancy Ahimsaa techniques.

The history of the Cellular Prison was depicted very well in the Hindi movie Kaalaapaanee showing the appalling conditions in that notorious prison. There was also the reference to one of the more famous interns of that prison, Shri VEER Savarkar. In recent times the name of Savarkar has attained political overtones due to his RSS affiliations back in those times. It is true that Savarkar did really brave deeds during his escape from a British ship docked in France. It is equally true that he was a daring young man who took the fight into the British camp, as a revolutionary freedom fighter in Maharashtra. However, he made the cardinal blunder of seeking clemency from the British Raj to send him back home from the cellular jail in the Andamans. There are many theories involved in this controversial subject.

One theory says that apart from writing periodic letters to the British, Savarkar's wife has also petitioned his captors on various occasions. It appears that the extremely harsh treatment in the cellular jail was becoming unbearable for Savarkar and hence his petitions. However the test of a true revolutionary is how much hardships he can take from his adversaries. It appears that Savarkar's soft upbringing was not able to hold him in good stead during his prison days. The controversy assumed political overtones when the opposition parties recently opposed the erection of his photo in the parliament building, branding him a coward. This is rather unfortunate. Certain political parties have gone out of the way to show that savarakar and Netaji Bose had a close relationship during the freedom struggle. This is not true at all, since Bose distanced himself both from the RSS (Arya Samaj) as well as the Muslim League. Bose stated that since both these political parties were religiously communal, he wanted no truck with either party. Bose had always stated that his party, the Forward Block and his INA were extremely secular organizations that welcomed all Indians into its fold, including Muslims, Christians, Hindus, Sikhs and Buddhists. Moreover both the RSS and the Muslim League supported the call for the partition of India, which Bose was dead against. Netaji Bose believed in a united India and warned many times that partition would only weaken our country and give rise to future troubles that would be unsolvable. And that's exactly what we are facing with Pakistan and China today on our land borders.

The first thing that Bose did on landing in Andamans was to form the office of the Azad Hind Government of exile in Port Blair, the capital of this island chain. He nominated commander Loganathan as the lt.Governor of his exile government on the Islands,sending a strong message to the world that his government was consolidating from Singapore to Port Blair. The selection of Cdr. Loganathan was also not by accident, since Bose wanted someone who knew the local language and culture to run his show. Since Cdr. Loganathan was of Tamil origin and the local language on the Islands was both Tamil and Bengali, it made it logical for him to be the chief. Bose intended to us these Islands as the launching pad of his fledging INA Navy with the help of the Japanese, who naval powers were well known to the wide world.

Bose had a very strong bondage with the Tamil people, who constituted almost 60% of his entire INA. The Andaman Islands had a large population of Tamil and Bengalee speaking folks s ince there was periodic sea travel between Madras port in southern India and also Calcutta port in undivided Bengal. Bose built an excellent rapport with the Andaman locals knowing very well that their support was important to keep the British at bay. He travelled the length and breath of this wonderfully large and beautiful Archipelego. He acquainted himself to the various native tribes present in the smaller Islands dotting this picturesque chain, especially the native negro tribes who resembled the African Aborigines. Bose realized that the capture of the Andaman Islands had a positive, psychological effect on the INA troos. Strategically, the Andaman Islands represented a launching pad for a future INA naval force to recapture the Indian mainland, starting with Chennai and Calcutta, which were the closest major Indian ports to port Blair, the exixsting naval base on these Islands. Moreover, it's a geographical fact that the Arakan coast of western Burma was much closer to the Andaman Islands than the eastern coast of India.

Netaji Bose had always believed in the total Cultural Unification of India, given its large topography, mixed relgions, caste ratios, language differences all over, etc. He realized that the only way that India could truly unite under One Flag was to first raise a common language. For this his policy was to retain Hindi as a verbal national language, however he wanted to use the Latin letters of the English language as a common script for all Indians. Daring as his policy appeared, he took this decision based on the complexity of India having more than 50 major languages and scores of dialects without any script. He chose English, simply because it was the official language of communication under the British administration of India. His economic policies for India was based on the socialist model of Russia around the second world war. Having travelled extensively into Europe, Bose found that the capitalistic models of America and Britain did not really help the common man of these countries.

## 9. The Burma Campaign

The INA went into battle during the Burma campaign of the invading Japanese army, since the first leg of the attack up the Malayan Peninsula was mostly over by the time the INA mobilized from Singapore upwards. Directly entering the jungles of Burma, the INA was given charge of specific operational areas to kick the British over the India border. Netaji Bose organized the various brigades of the INA to specific sectors of the battles under his trusted officers like Col. Mohammed Kiani, Col.Sehgal, Col. Dhillon and Col.Shah Nawaz khan. Many of the troops were largely inexperienced being raw hands who had volunteered based on the clarion call of Bose. But some of the INA soldiers and officers were battle-hardened POWs, who had seen recent action in the British-Indian army, fighting against the German, Japanese and Italian armies in Europe, Asia and Africa. These Indian POWs showed remarkable leadership skills in training and motivating these raw recruits to handle weapons and also on the art of warfare.

The INA won sporadic victories in battle against the British Army in Burma, inspite of shortage in weapons, ammunition, food supplies and medicine. Considering the INA was purely a voluntary army without a salary, the motivation level of the troops was purely patriotism alone. They were pitted against the British-Indian army comprising well-paid and well-fed mercenary Indian soldiers, many of whom were unaware that they were firing at their own compatriots in the INA. Many of them thought they were fighting only the Japanese army in Burma, but when they counted the dead among their enemy, they found soldiers of Indian origin. The news blackout within the British army was so total that their soldiers had no idea what was going on around the outside world. It was only after the end of the war in south-east Asia, that both sides realized that they had inadvertently killed their own friends and relatives of Indian origin on opposite sides of the war.

There can be no doubt that if only Gandhi had not supported the British during the second world war by allowing Indians to join as soldiers in the British army, India would have attained independence much before 1947. The entire war in Europe, Asia and Africa was fought by Indian soldiers reporting to British officers. The total count of Indian soldiers who participated in the 6-year second world war was 2.5 million troops. These troops were considered one of the most obedient and subservient troops of the entire British army world wide. And they were excellent fighters and military workmen as attested by the German, Italian and Japanese officers who fought against them. Field Marshal Erwin Rommel has repeatedly stressed in many interviews that if it hadn't been for the Fourth Indian Division, the Germans would have won the North African military campaign.

Instead of demanding the Indian soldiers in the British army to quit immediately upon the commencement of the second world war in September 1939, Gandhi made the cardinal mistake of encouraging more and more Indian citizens to the enlist in the British army, just to keep Hitler at bay. The blunder was not realized until the Indian soldiers of the British 14th Army locked horns with the INA troops fighting alongside the Japanese army in Burma. It was then that it became a tragedy, as Indians started killing their own friends and relatives across enemy lines without knowing whom they were shooting at. The Press Censorship was so strong in India and within the British army during the second world war that the Indian troops were not even aware that the INA had joined hands with the Japanese army in Burma. Hence it was a complete shock for them to see INA troops dead or wounded after they were captured as POWs. However the INA was fully aware they were taking on Indian troops in the British army, since it was standard practice by Britain for the last 150 years. Hence the INA had a propaganda unit just to throw posters and handbills on the British troops asking them to join the INA and fight for their motherland. Even loudspeakers were used from a safe distance tempting Indian troops to cross over to the INA side in Burma.

In one of the most difficult acts during the Burma campaign, the INA troops manning one side of the massive Irrawady river in central Burma, kept the advancing British forces at bay for more than two days. The INA machine gun units were small and scattered across one bank while the British forces were larger and more well equipped on the opposite bank. But the sheer dedication of the INA troops coupled with accurate fire kept the enemy pegged down without any advancement. The British found this situation extremely bogging down on their operations that it was finally brought to the notice of General

William Slim, the commander of the British 14th army in Burma. Finally Slim had to personally request the Royal Air Force to intervene to neutralize the INA machine gunners. Only after 2 RAF fighter aircraft attacked the INA positions, could the British cross the river to continue their forward thrust. Even today there are military academies across the world that take the example of the INA as a successful Guerilla army that stayed the long arm of the British empire in South East Asia. Some of the best jungle Guerilla armies in the world, including the Vietnam and Cuban armies, have learnt extensively from the INA tactics and used them against their enemies.

Much later the organization called the Liberation Tigers of Tamil EELAM or in short simply as LTTE, which fought a long lasting civil war against the Sri Lankan army, owed its tactics and inspiration to Netaji Bose and his INA. During many war time interviews with the world media during the 1980s and 1990s, including TIME and BBC, the LTTE supremo Mr. Prabhakaran has openly called Netaji Bose as his role model and inspiration to form the LTTE. So impressed was he by Bose's patriotism and military vision that he directly copied two important aspects of the INA into his LTTE. First, he adopted the very same INA springing Tiger flag for the LTTE. Likewise he formed a ladies army unit very similar to the Rani Jhansi Regiment of the INA, which he called the Black Tigers. This unit distinguished itself in battle against the Sri Lankan army. The members of this unit were hand picked by Prabhakaran himself to ensure he got only deeply motivated female cadres.

The Burma campaign, though initially a success for the marauding Japanese army coupled with the INA, ran into trouble during the final stages as the war approached the Indian border. Around that time the Battle of Midway, a major Naval battle ,had just taken place between the American and Japanese Navy in the southern Pacific Ocean. The Japanese suffered a huge loss of battle-trained men and material that was difficult to replace and recoup. They lost many of their battle ships and destroyers to the American Navy, which suffered relatively smaller casualties. This defeat put a huge strain on the Japanese government and the financial and trained manpower losses were heavy. Hence funds that were supposed to reach South East Asia was diverted to the protection of the homeland, Japan itself, against air attack from the American air force and Navy. This financial crunch effected the INA directly since precious weapons and war materials stopped coming to the Burma front. Even much needed medical supplies and food rations came down to a trickle. During the second half of the entire Burma campaign, as the INA retreated into interior Burma from the Indian border, the casualty rate was high. Not from British bullets, but from starvation, lack of medical supplies and tropical diseases. The INA lost close to 30,000 troops due to the above reasons in the jungles of South East Asia. One of the highest military attrition rates in the second world war was experienced by the INA, not because of gun shot wounds but due to starvation and disease. Certainly nothing to be proud about, especially since the INA was a purely voluntary army without wages or salary paid out.

The INA distinguished itself in battle in various sectors in Burma including Mount Popa, Tammu, Irawaddy delta, Mandalay, Rangoon, Arakans, etc. Many war historians, both Indian and foreign, have lauded the bravery of the INA troops in battle against the British army in the Burma campaign. Even though the INA consisted of quite a few irregular civilians who were fighting an organized war for the first time, the bravery and fearlessness exhibited by them was outstanding. For example, the INA did not retreat in many of the fierce battles fought in the steamy jungles of Malaya and Burma, rather they stood their ground and only against overwhelming odds did the capitulate to the enemy troops. British historian Hugh Toye in his book on Netaji Bose and the INA has very clearly mentioned that the INA gave a splendid display of its fighting prowess in south-east Asia by its relentless pursuit of British troops retreating to India across the Burma border. Even during the retreat of the INA into Burma from India, immediately after the Imphal and Kohima disasters, the INA gave a good account of itself by strategically withdrawing deeper into southern Burma, back to Singpapore, via Malaya.

One of the challenges that faced the British-American troops stationed in India was to keep the supply routes open to Chinese Guerilla troops fighting the Japanese army in the southern China province of Yunnan, bordering the Northern Burmese province of Shan. The supply route in use was to fly American transport aircraft over the eastern Himalayas across India's North East Frontier Agency or simply called NEFA. Today India has renamed NEFA as its frontier state of Arunachal Pradesh. American transport planes used to take off from Calcutta, flying at a high altitude over the eastern Himalayas and land in the town of Kunming, which was the capital of Yunnan. As flying over this air route, popanary called as "The Hump" involved these heavy transport aircraft to negotiate the high Himalayan ranges of north-eastern India, the American troops stationed in India were looking at a safer land route to maintain essential supplies to the Chinese Guerilla fighters. The Americans embarked on building a highway cutting acroos north-eastern India and Northern Burma directly into the Chinese province of Yunnan. The project was named the Stilwell Road Project in honour of Col. Joe Stilwell of the American corps of engineers stationed in India.

Work on the project got off in right earnest from the Indian side, but ran into difficulties once it entered Northern Burma, where the Burmese Guerillas fighting with the Japanese army against the British troops kept attacking the road project. However with great difficulty the Americans completed this road project linking north eastern India with southern China, via Northern Burma. However the utility of this Stilwell Road reduced considerably after the defeat of the Japanese-INA combine in the battles of Imphal and also Kohima. Once the retreat of the Japs and INA back to central Burma started, the pressure on Northern Burma eased considerably and the supplies to the Chinese Guerillas stopped. For our information, these Chinese Guerillas were the troops of the Koumintang, the Chinese political party controlling southern China in the mid-1940s under the leadership of Mr. Sun Yet San. Even though the Americans and British supported this political faction, it was the Communist party under the leadership of Mr. Mao Zedong that finally defeated the Koumintang troops and drove them out of mainland China to the neighbouring island of Taipei, now known as Taiwan. The communist party under their forces called as the People's Liberation Army or PLA, swept through the entire China mainland and established their government in 1949. The next year this same PLA troops invaded Tibet and annexed it within a few years, with neighbouring India standing and watching mutely.

It is important for modern India to note the status of our peaceful neighbour Burma, then and now. Burma is a Buddhist country and they have gratitude that India is the land that gave them Buddhism. Burma till today has never had a territorial dispute with India, which is amazing, since most of India's neighbours are having a territorial dispute with us. During the British occupation of India and Burma, the town of Mandalay in central Burma was infamous for its central jail that was used to house political prisoners, including freedom fighter from India. One of its famous inmates in the 1930s was Netaji Bose, who contacted Tubercolosis after being interred in Mandalay Jail. The TB was so bad that Bose lost one lung to this communicable disease and had to be sent back to India by the British authorities fearing he would die in prison. So Bose had already had a taste of Burma, before his INA marched through its jungles fighting the British troops. His experiences in Mandalay was remembered when during the INA march across Burma, he visited the grave of the last Mughal Indian emperor of India Mohammed Shah Zafar, who died in prison after being arrested and sent out of India for life imprisonment in Mandalay central prison. This was an act of secularism since Bose believed that only the combined unity of both Hindus and Muslims in India could ever bring freedom from Britain.

Netaji Bose had excellent relations with the famous freedom fighter of Burma, Shri Aung Sang, who is the Father of the Nation for Burma. Both of them were supported by the invading Japanese army against the British administration. It is pertinent to note that the daughter of Aung Sang is the present Prime Minister of Burma Mrs. Aung Sang Syu Kyi, who had been toppled by the Burmese military Junta in 2021 after winning the democratic national elections with a huge mandate. It is even more pertinent to note that India, being the largest working democracy in the world has done practically nothing to oppose the brutal regime of the military Junta, which has repeatedly seized power by toppling the democratically elected governments, time and again. The silence of such a large democratic country like ours standing silent when a neighbouring country is brutalized by a cruel dictatorship does not augur well for the world. One must remember that this inhuman dictatorship Junta had earlier kept Mrs. Syu Kyi under house arrest for extended periods of time and even denied her permission to visit her ailing husband in England, after which he eventually passed away. Even upon his death, she did not go for his funeral abroad, fearing she would not be allowed to re-enter Burma again.

Today as the Burmese opposition forces unite under a common military Guerilla force with mass local involvement, India has not taken any stance to support democracy. On the contrary China has moved her ships for a joint naval exercise with the military junta, whom they are indirectly supporting. The Norther Burmese state of Shan, bordering China, has fallen to the opposition Guerilla army. The western state of Rakhine on the Arakan coast is collapsing to the rebel army. All India has to do is to move her army to consolidate the position of the rebel forces so that the military junta is slowly but surely kicked out of power. This will also send a message to China that India is interested in restoring democracy in Burma, no matter what the cost is. It is truly a tragedy that India has done precious little to help Burma that has been reeling under sporadic military dictatorships for more than two decades. This could be the golden opportunity for India to support the democratic movement in Burma, before the Chinese reassert themselves by grabbing the strategic Burmese ports and cities, thereby making difficult for outside intervention. It is totally shocking that such a large democratic nation like ours has done precious little to support democracy in neighbouring Burma.

# 10. Flag Hoisting at Moirang

The INA created history when its troops crossed the Burmese border into Indian territory in the village of Moirang in Manipur and hoisted the tricolor on 14th April, 1944 ,under the leadership of Col. Shaukath Mallik. The dream of Netaji Bose and the entire INA happened like magic. The British army put up strong resistance to both the Japanese army and the INA, knowing very well that it would be a psychological booster for the INA to enter Indian soil. But the entry of the INA into Indian soil could not be denied, as the INA wave finally broke through the British cordon. Celebrations broke out within the rank and file of the INA and the news spread like wildfire to the Singapore headquarters and then on to the Japanese High Command in Tokyo. However the cunning British withheld this pathbreaking news from the public in India, fearing there would be an upheaval and revolution. Using the draconian Official Secrets Act and the Military Act, the British suppressed all the developments of the Burma campaign from the Indian citizens.

Moirang was a turning point in the war in South East Asia as it signified a full, round trip around the world for the leader of the INA, Shri Netaji Subash Chandra Bose. Three years ago this same person had left India through its North Western border in disguise, crossed three continents to finally renter India in full military uniform as the commander of its free Army through her North Eastern border. Here was a person who swore he would plant the flag of free India on her sacred soil with his independent army and on that fateful day he achieved his goal with the help of an ebullient Army of dedicated volunteer soldiers. Here was an intellectual genius who stood at all India 4th rank in the coveted Indian Civil Services (ICS) exams and yet chose to resign from this service to take up the yoke of attaining freedom for India, building an army at a relatively young age.

That the national tricolor was hoisted in the North-eastern corner of India is a standing testimony to the multi-cultural nation that comprises India. While Bose exited India in the North-western corner of India, he reappeared on the North-eastern corner, proving to the British that he could move all over his motherland without getting their express permission. The speed with which Bose moved around the world after exiting India in 1941, still baffles historians and military experts alike. Here was a man with no formal military training, yet was able to plan and execute his travel and strategy with meticulous precision down to the last detail. Here was a man who quit his exalted public position as one of the pillars of the Congress Party just to travel third class, all over the world, to attain freedom for his motherland. Netaji Bose inspired the formal independence of not just his motherland India, but also many countries of south and South East Asia, including Burma, Malaysia, Singapore, Philipines, Indonesia, Combodia, Vietnam, Laos, Thailand, Brunie, etc. This is popularly called the Domino Effect and Bose with his characteristic charisma and empathy to countries suffering under imperialsm, was able to create the Independence Wave in both Asia and Africa.

The success of the INA in entering Indian soil after grouping in faraway Singapore, inspired the freedom struggle of nations as diverse as Cuba and Vietnam. The Cuban hero, Fidel Castro, has often mentioned that though he considered Gandhi as the leader of the Indian freedom struggle, he still felt that it was Subash Bose that broke the back of the British empire in India. In an interview with a foreign press correspondent, Castro says he had drawn inspiration from the INA when he formed his own Guerilla band of warriors trying to overthrow the dictatorship of Fulgencio Bastista in Cuba, way back in the late 1950s. He said that the organizational skills of Bose outside India was stupendous and he drew lessons from them and applied it to the Cuban freedom struggle. When Castro's team of 80 members assembled in nearby Mexico, was reduced to just 10 members after being hit by the government forces, he drew strength from the INA who made the choice of retreating back into Burma rather than surrender to the British forces. Castro also learnt many Guerilla tactics form the INA, used in the jungle warfare of Burma and Malaya against the British army.

These jungle warfare tactics of the INA were also studied by the Viet-Cong under the leadership of Ho Chi-Minh during their epic 2 decades of resistance against the American occupational forcey in Vietnam. Of course, the vietcong went one better and used a vast network of underground caves to create havoc behind the enemy American troops. The Vietnam war will always be remembered as a war that tested the grit of a nation under siege from a world super-power called America.

One of the most iconic warriors of the recent decades is most certainly our Che Guevera, who was deputy to his supreme commander, Fidel Castro during the 1959 Cuban revolution. During an interview, to a foreign press correspondent in the early 1960s, Che has mentioned Subash Bose as an unsung hero of the Indian freedom movement. Che clearly stated that though the world looks at Gandhi as the father of Indian freedom, it was Bose and his INA that contributed to victory on the ground for Indian independence. Che clearly stated that both Fidel and himself learnt many lessons from the organizational genius of Bose struggling to cobble together a native Indian army in a foreign land. The Cuban revolution was similarly planned and executed in Mexico, due to its natural animosity to America, which was imperialistically dominating Cuba, manipulating its dictatorship under Fulgencio Batista. Frequent trips across the Gulf of Mexico were required before Fidel Castro's band of daring revolutionaries established a bridgehead in Cuba. This small band of revolutionaries trained in Mexico grew into the revolutionary army which finally stormed Havana city to declare independence from the American-backed dictatorship. in many ways, the Cuban revolution succeeded in ultmate military victory as compared to the INA which lost the crucial battles of Imphal and Kohima. However, the INA finally achieved Indian independence through the turmoil it created with the Red Fort Trials.

During the American invasion and occupation of Vietnam, the technologically superior American army was forced to slow down and finally exit Vietnam after close to 20 years of military conflict. The main reason was that the Viet Cong army used improvised Guerilla tactics in the jungles which the American army was unable to contain. The Americans got so desperate that they finally resorted to chemical warfare by using Agent Orange to defoliate large patches of jungle through helicopters. Even today, this is considered an international crime against humanity since many thousands of Vietnamese villagers living near the forests were sprayed with the chemical, even though the target were the jungle trees overhead. Many villagers died and others suffered third degree burns and skin cancer which was also transmitted genetically to their children. During the war, the leader of the Viet Cong, Mr. Ho Chi Mihn, had clearly stated that many of the jungle warfare tactics used were learnt from the INA, which had a presence not only in Malaya and Burma, but also in Siam (now Thailand) and Indo-China (now Vietnam). He was full of praise for Subash Bose, whom he referred to the father of the freedom movement of not just his native India, but also most of the south-east Asian countries including

Vietnam. Ho Chi Mihn stated that one of the inspirations to fight back against the American imperial army was not only Fidel Castro of Cuba but also Subash Bose of India. He said just as Fidel took on the armed might of the super-power American-backed military junta in Cuba and subsequently wresting control of Cuba, so also he was immensely inspired by Bose who took on the might of the British empire with all its military might with a small army of his own.

Ho Chi Mihn further stated that he was shocked at how history repeated itself, sometimes without rhyme or reason. For example, it was the same British empire that once invaded America in the late 1770s. The local American citizens banded together under a small army under George Washington and finally kicked out the British army. Even after remaining an independent democracy for close to 200 years, the Americans became invading imperialists themselves, poking their noses into many countries of Asia and Africa in the late 1940s until the present times. Thus Ho chi Mihn referred to the Americans as the worst hypocrites of the 20th century. America claimed to be the world's most efficient democracy, yet continued to invade countries all round the world, mostly for financial gain. The country that prided itself in its democratic charter is today the world's worst oppressor. The more recent examples of Somalia, Afghanistan, Iraq and Syria are all there for us to see and shake our heads in disgust.

The flag hoisting at Moirang has a special message for the India of today. A huge country like India needs to physically assimilate its peoples, especially the ones that live in the remote corners like the North-East. Today as some parts of north and west India behave with a superiority complex toward the migrant labour from the North-East, we need to learn lessons on why Netaji Bose chose to enter India across Burma. Bose never considered any corner of India as too remote or inaccessible. When he crossed the hostile region of the Khyber into Afghanistan, he never felt awkward or afraid. He mixed freely with the rough Pathans of the Khyber region with native competence. He also moved very smoothly with the many tribal communities of Nagaland and Manipur, during the battles of Imphal and Kohima. Never once did he doubt that these remote regions denoted integral parts of India which needed close monitoring and Hand-holding. But in recent times, India has experienced very poor relationship with the north-east tribes since we consider them too primitive and backward. As a result many of these states of the north-east have developed animosity towards India and instead started slanting to China. This is an extremely dangerous situation since China is always looking at ways to destabilize India through the north east and Kashmir.

## 11. The Battle of Imphal

The turning point of the Burma campaign was indeed the Battle of Imphal. According to the Japanese army, this battle was supposed to be the mother of all battles to secure the Indian peninsula into Japanese hands. However, it turned out to be quite the opposite as the Japs had grossly underestimated the British army positions in the north-east. A combination of bad military intelligence, lack of air support, poor logistical support and the early arrival of the monsoons contributed to the defeat of the INA fighting alongside Japanese troops. The Imphal operations were supposed to herald the death knell of the imperial British troops in India. However the tragic turn of events went against the spirited battle performance of the INA, compounded by the over-confidence of the Japanese high command who had only partial military intelligence to support them. Instead of turning out to be the swan song of the British, the battle of Imphal turned out to be the Waterloo of the INA in south-east Asia.

Military historians are still at logger-heads to pin-point the exact reason for the Japanese debacle at Imphal. Many attribute it to Samurai arrogance among the upper echelons of the Japanese military high command in Burma. Others attribute it to the poor chain of command in the Japanese military in South East Asia. Some others put the blame on Gandhi for keeping silence even after knowing that the Indian soldiers of the British army in Imphal were being used against Indian soldiers of the INA. Instead of giving a clarion call for all Indian troops in the British army to lay down their arms, he openly kept silent which sent an open message that he had no objection to the INA being massacred by their fellow Indian soldiers in the British Indian army.

Many have questioned why Gandhi had allowed Indian soldiers to participate in the second world war under the command of the British army. Many historians had wondered how an Apostle of Peace like Gandhi could condone the use of Indian soldiers to join an armed war against Adolf Hitler by the British. Knowing fully well the British could not be trusted for any word of honour that they would quit India immediately after the second world war,

Gandhi was a silent spectator to the mass enlistment of Indian labout to join the British army. History will never forgive Gandhi for condoning the use of Indian manpower to be used as cannon-fodder against similar Indian soldiers of the INA.

The battle of Imphal also saw the use of Indian pilots by the British Royal Air Force to bombard both Japanese and INA troops along the entire Imphal-Dimapur corridor. During my visit to the Air Force Technical College in Bangalore a few years ago, I was regaled to the story of how the British were caught in a quandary on how to tackle the invading Japanese army entering Manipur through the Burma border. They badly needed their air force to attack the Japs in the air but did not have adequate aircraft nearby to support them. The nearest available fighter-bomber aircraft was located at Lahore in the north-west corner of undivided India. The challenge was to first make these ageing aircraft battle-ready and then fly them all the way across Northern India to the far north-east corner, a distance of close to 2000 kms. I was told that there were no British pilots available as they were also busy fighting in Europe against the German army. The onus fell on the Indian pilots to fly them, much against the wishes of the British high command, who had low confidence on the flying capabalities of Indian "coolie" pilots.

Since the situation at Imphal was very desperate for the defending British troops, admiral Mountbatten who was in charge of the south Asian operations of the second world war, ordered the Indian pilots to immediately fly to Manipur with a refueling halt in a Northern Indian air base. The Indian pilots scrambled at after a long haul flight they joined the battle of Imphal, literally with a bang. These ageing fighter-bomber British aircraft, including Spitfires and Hurricanes were used effectively to bomb and strafe key Japanese movements across the Burma border. In fact, it was the arrival of these airdraft that changed the tide of the battle, in favour of the British. The Japanese were hampered by total lack of air support while the British saved the day with their aerial bombardment. Many war historians and experts attribute a large part of the ultimate victory in the battle of Imphal to the British air support which grounded the Japanese troops and totally hampered Japanese advances into Indian territory.

As I went through the aircraft museum at the AFTC, Bangalore, I felt a twinge of bitterness that the British cunningly used Indian "coolie" pilots to bombard their own countrymen fighting in the INA alongside the Japanese army at the battle of Imphal. I was left with a bitter taste in my mouth at the feeling at how manipulative the British were and how cleverly they used Indians to fight Indians. And all this happened under the very eyes of Mr. Gandhi, the apostle of non-violence. The question remains, was Gandhi an passive spectator to the genocide that was enacted at both the battles of Imphal and Kohima in mid-1944?

## 12. The battle of Kohima

One of the bloodiest battles ever fought in the second world war was not fought in Europe or Africa. It was fought in Asia, that too in the land of the saint of non-voilence, Mr. Gandhi. Today Kohima is a large town in India which is also the capital of the state of Nagaland. Around 80 years ago, Kohima was a small border town adjoining Burma, now Myanmar. What started as a small battle between the defending British troops and the invading Japanese troops turned into a full fledged blood bath on both sides. A small contingent of Japanese troops surrounding the British governor's bunglow in Kohima and attempted to take the incumbent British troops captive. The British troops resisted stoutly and in fact brought in reinforcement with LMG support. The Governor's bunglow was nestled on a hillock in Kohima and a large tennis court demarcated the gap between the two forces. Sensing early victory the Japs moved in for the kill, but were met with highly accurate machine gun fire and had to take cover.

With more and more reinforcements arriving for the British troops from their hinterland base, the Japs requested for more of their own reinforcement and additional LMG and MMG units. The INA also pitched in along with the Japs and it became a total fire fight. The casualty figure on both sides rose by the hour and Kohima earned the dubious distinction of hosting a river of blood for that fateful two weeks of pitched battle. This battle turned out to be a perfect Battle of Attrition, with neither side willing to ask or give a quarter. A fight to the finish, the battle of Kohima also marked the final turning point for the INA in its Burma campaign. With supplies running low, both food and medicine, the Japs and the accompanying INA suffered massive casualties. Most of the casualties were from bullet injuries since there was almost zero stock of important medical supplies. Many of the Japs and INA troops died of septic wounds, gangrene and blood poisoning. Many died of starvation, which was truly a crying shame given that the INA was a voluntary organisation and the least the higher command could do was to provide food to their troops which were not being paid otherwise. The news that many of his troops had died of starvation in the battle field left Netaji Bose in tears. He realized that these men of his had given their everything to the motherland and on his part he was unable to influence the Japs to maintain regular food supplies.

Since the source of food supplies from the Japanese army had died down, Bose ordered his troops to buy food from the surrounding villages in Burma and within the Indian border. Many of the villagers from the Naga tribes were willing to part with food for the INA troops, only that they had deep reservations about the Japanese soldiers who sometimes behaved very crudely with them. Many times the villagers used to be hesitant since they had already been warned by the earlier British administration that if they supported the enemy with food supplies, action would be taken once the British came back to power. However with the voice of Netaji Bose being played on speakers in these villages, requesting for food and rations, many villagers were convinced that their loyalaties lay with the INA, who had come to liberate them from foreign, imperial powers. The INA authorities made sure to pay the villagers in cash, sometimes in kind and very rarely on credit during emergencies. At no point did the INA demand or threaten the villagers for food and other essential supplies, as per the express orders of their supreme commander, Shri Netaji Bose.

Kohima was vital in the defence of the Brahmaputra valley in Assam, as once this town fell, the nearby town of Dimapur would be open for attack. Dimapur was the end of the highlands and the beginning of the plains, where the major roads and railway lines converged for bringing in vital supplies for the British troops of the Burma campaign. The battle of Kohima was a disaster for the Japanese and the INA, chiefly because they ran out of food and medical supplies. Even important artillery and tank power coupled with air support was solely lacking for the Japanese. The British enjoyed all these three components of the war since the Assam Valley served as a conduit for troops and supplies from the Indian subcontinent. The battle of Kohima also saw a major showdown between two senior officers of the Japanese army on how much to penetrate into India. This showdown led to a lot of unnecessary confusion on the major strategies to be followed during the course of the battle. However even British historians have acknowledged that the Japanese and the INA fought exceptionally well with no backup support. In fact after the battle, the Japanese camp resembled a mortuary where the Japs fought to the finish in true Samurai style, all guns blazing. Many soldiers had died of starvation, disease and bullet injuries due to total lack of supplies. That is why the battle of Kohima is often dubbed by war historians as the Stalingrad Of The East.

## 13. Retreat to Singapore

As the INA and Japanese army were defeated in the two critical battles of Imphal and Kohima, they had no option but to retreat back to Burma. The Japanese refused to lay down arms locally in the true spirit of the Samurai tradition that prefers suicide to surrender. Netaji Bose had to take a call to surrender, but in the true spirit of the Indian Kshatriya warrior, he opted for the INA to fight on till ultimate capitulation. As the INA supreme commander, Bose had the option of being airlifted by the Japaenese army back to Rangoon, but opted instead to manually retreat along with the Rani Jhansi Womens Regiment which was carrying the mobile field hospital and medical supplies. Bose also felt indebted to the women troops of the INA, as they had taken so much personal sacrifice to form the Jhansi Rani Regiment against all odds. Hence he decided to march back to Burma along with the ladies regiment, knowing this route would be slow and dangerous.

Burma was a large country criss-crossed by rivers and the monsoon was a very tricky time to fight a war. One of the main reasons that historians have alluded to the defeat of the Indo-Japanese forces in Burma, was the onset of early monsoon rains in the end of May 1944 itself. Rains that struck every year mid-June, advanced itself in 1944 and dealt a cruel blow to the Japanese war effort alongside the INA. Just when the national flag had been hoisted on 14th April in Moirang and the euphoria was burning in the INA camp for having entered holy Indian soil, did the monsoon set in and smashed up the logistical dreams of the Japs and INA. During the incessant monsoon rains, all the jungle tracks turned to quagmire and muddy pits. Heavy vehicles like military trucks simply couldn't move, since they often got stuck in the soggy mud tracks and caused traffic jams for all other vehicles coming behind them. Moreover these trucks and battle tanks became Sitting Ducks for British aircraft that were hovering in the area searching for Japanese road transport targets to bomb away.

Moreover, the entire area became leach infected and most of the INA soldiers trekking in the Burmese jungles were fair game for the leeches lurking in the undergrowth. These leeches got inside the soldiers uniforms and boots, sucking blood and generally making themselves a nuisance by blood staining the entire area. Adding to the woes of the INA troops was the presence of malaria in the jungles of Burma. Being a monsoon region, rain water often stagnated in the crevices and cracks of large trees, encouraging the breeding of mosquitoes that required these stagnant pools of water for dropping their eggs. Malaria was a huge threat for the INA troops and many suffered high fever in the jungles which often proved fatal since there was a shortage of anti-malarial drugs during the war in Burma. It is estimated that the INA lost hundreds of troops to malaria alone.

The next big killer was dysentery. With the rivers and streams of Burma getting contaminated due to the large influx of humans during the war, dysentery was endemic. With shortage of clean, portable water most of the troops were forced to drink untreated river water which often transmitted bacterial diseases like cholera, typhoid and dysentery. It is estimated that many hundreds of INA troops lost their lives to water-borne diseases. The shortage of medicines further complicated the health of the troops and many died due to the untimely arrival of critical medicine, including anti-biotics, drips, pain-killers as well as Penicillin. It a bitter truth of the Burma campaign that the INA troops starved to death and died of their injuries due to shortage of medicine more than to the bullets of the British army. During the war when Bose was personally visiting the field hospitals in the jungle campaigns against the British army, he was personally mortified on seeing the plight of his injured troops who succumbed to secondary wound infections due to shortage of basic drugs. Inspite of the best nursing care provided by the dedicated lady soldiers of the Jhansi Rani Regiment, many of the INA troops could not survive and died painful deaths due to lack of antibiotics and pain killers.

One of the deaths that personally traumatized Netaji Bose was the death of Lt.Nazeer to his mortal wounds. The nurses of the Medical Corps worked night and day for over 3 days trying to save his life, but were unsuccessful. It was all the more heart rending since Lt.Nazeer was a young INA army officer well liked by his unit, both seniors and juniors. Bose spent one full night in the camp hospital waiting for news of the recovery of Nazeer, but in vain. Nazeer's untimely death left a void in the INA lower leadership, since he always led from the front and had a reputation of being of high valour. The news of his death was taken by much sadness and also brought home the point to both Indians and foreigners alike that the INA was truly a secular army that had volunteer soldiers from all religions and castes of India, including Hindu, Muslim, Christian, Sikh and Buddhist. Nazeer's death also brought home that point that medical supplies were running out and hence the mortality rate of the INA troops were increasing day by day. Inspite of the best efforts of commander Bose, the Japanese were unable to keep both the food and medical supplies in sufficient quantities thus leading to the unwarranted deaths of many INA soldiers and officers. However the fault did not lie with the local Japanese army administration but to the fact that the government in Japan had become cash strapped due to the immense war expenditure all over Asia. One of the main causes for their financial losses was the defeat of the Japanese navy in the Battle of Midway which took a heavy toll on the ships and other naval infrastructure of the Japanese. Not only did Japan lose precious aircraft carriers, destroyers and battle-ships, they also lost irreplaceable lives in the form of experienced naval officers, sailors and technical personnel. This was a huge strain on the Japanese war effort and financial aid to the Burmese campaign dwindled considerably leading to the deaths by starvation of both INA and Japanese troops.

Many INA troops were forced to surrender on the retreat back to Singapore from Burma. Many of the INA troops were dispersed across different locations in western Burma after the Imphal disaster and hence took multiple routes to go south towards Malaya and Singapore. Some INA troops, including capt. Laxmi was capture in the Mabaw valley where the had taken refuge for a few weeks in the dense jungles. However the local Burmese tribals informed the British army of their whereabouts and one fine day the INA figutives were ambushed by the local British-Indian army. Lack of equipment and machinery was also a major problem for the retreating INA troops. Shortage of fuel and rations further complicated the situation. Those who criticized the failure of the INA to win the Burma campaign, forgot that the formation of the INA itself was a herculean effort by Netaji Bose. They even forgot that the INA was a purely Voluntary Army that did not give salary or any other financial incentive to its soldiers or officers. The motivating factor for these INA troops was pure patriotism. To that measure, the INA was a resounding success and with the famous Red Fort Trials and the decisive Naval Mutiny broke the back of the mighty British empire in India and forced the sun to finally set on this collapsing imperial power.

## 14. Atomic Bombs and Surrender

The Japanese army continued the war in South East Asia, even after the surrender of Germany in early May 1945. The war in Europe had ended but Asia was still burning with the ebullient Japs giving the British army a run for its money. The japs were unwilling to stop the war in the pacific ocean against the Americans, even when they started getting bombed in their home soil. President Roosevelt was under pressure to end the bloody war and along came an excuse in the name of the Atom Bomb. On August 6, 1945, an American long range bomber dropped a mysterious bomb on the city of Hiroshima in the early hours of the morning. The bomb exploded in a fury of fire and brimstone, causing fire storms to spontaneously ignite. Many of the citizens were burnt to death and those who survived had radiation burns all over them. This was the consequence of the world's first Atom Bomb being dropped on an enemy nation and Japan was the first ginuea pig to experience the same. For the first time, nuclear radiation was experienced by the Japanese people and it was really scary with future generations being born with all kinds of genetic disorders. The total death toll of the first atomic bombing of Hiroshima was close to one lakh.

The American expectation of an immediate Japanese surrender did not transpire and hence the Americans decided to go for a bigger atomic bomb dropping. In the early hours of August 9th, another long range bomber dropped a bigger atom bomb on the city of Nagasaki, creating untold miseries for its polulation. Many thousands more died, but this time the Japanese government immediately surrendered due to the pressure of the entire nation. It is widely believed that the Americans were actually testing their atomic bombs to establish their supremacy as a major military power. It is also widely believed that the Japs had actually offered to surrender immediately after the first atomic bombing on 6th August, but the Americans pretended not to understand their overtures on purpose. Historians are of the view that the Americans were on the winning path and did not have to use an atomic weapon to end the war. Some historians feel the American government wanted to test these weapons for their strategic interest and hence the act of dropping these two atom bombs was premature and dangerous.

With the surrender of Japan to America, the onus on Netaji Bose became clearer. Being a military partner of the Japanese army, he had to make a quick decision to surrender or to fight on. After consulting his senior colleagues in the INA, Bose decided to surrender, since without Japanese logistical support, the war was as good as over. Moreover, the British being vastly superior to the INA in both personnel and weapons, Bose knew that continuing the war would involve immense casualities to his troops, who had already suffered enough in the jungles of Burma and Malaya. With a heavy heart, on August 11th ,1945, Netaji Bose, as the head of the Indian Government in exile announced a formal cease-fire with the British troops in Singapore.

One must also understand that the Japanese, before their surrender, were now fighting a lonely battle against the combined Allies which included America, Britain and Russia. Their original allies in the Axis club used to be Germany and Italy. It was the Italians who surrendered first to exit the club, when the allies invaded Rome. The next to leave were the Germans as soon as Berlin fell to the invading Russian forces. And finally, the Japanese were all alone. Yet they chose to fight to the finish despite being left without any support. That's when the Americans decided to fire-bomb the towns and cities of Japan mercilessly. Knowing that the japs were on the back-foot due to economic and finanacial constraints, the Americans decided to turn the knife by pounding Japanese territory day and night. Meanwhile the American scientists were busy at work on the atomic bomb which was at completion stage. Yet it had never been really tested and the Japanese provided perfect target practice for a country that never forgave the Pearl Harbour Bombings. Inspite of saner voices within his government and scholars advising the use of weapons of mass destruction on innocent civilians, president Harry Trueman decided to test the bombs on a hapless Japanese public. And so it was that these two bombs called Little Boy and Fat Man were loaded on to the long range bombers to drop them over Hiroshima and Nagasaki in early august 1945. This act of American will always be remembered for its selfish intentions, namely to test the weapons in the battle field as also to announce to the world that they were the new super powers.

There was pandemonium in Japan as all hell broke loose after the bombings. Mass graves had to be dug while many civilians suffered third degree burns from the massive fires that followed the mushroom cloud explosion. Radiation from these bombs were about to infect an entire generation and more. The unthinkable happened as the whole world looked on including the allies of America, which included Britain and Russia. The beginning of the Cold War had just begun, as the Russians began to suspect the Americans of hegemony in the war against the Nazis and the Fascists. The dropping of the atom bombs began the arms race which culminated in the establishment of the bi-polar world, headed by America and Russia.

# 15. Asylum in Russia

The surrender of the Japanese dilemma. Hitherto the Japanese and the Germans had given complete logistic and material support for the INA and now the future looked bleak for them. The surrender of Japan meant that henceforth none of the captured territories of Japan was safe to remain in, any more. Any person or material staying in these territories could immediately be arrested or confisicated respectively by the victorious British and American armies. The British and American forces were just one day's journey form Taiwan, where Netaji had halted enroute to his proposed journey to Manchuria from Saigon.

Bose was in a dilemma as to where he would go for shelter, now that Japan had surrendered and all her Asian territories would now fall into the hands of the British and Americans.d There was absolutely no way Bose could go back to India where he was a wanted man by the ruling British Raj. He could make a dash for Africa, but then British secret agents were teeming around in Asia and Africa. South America was unheralded territory and would be too risky since American double agents could be operating from Mexico and keeping a close watch for foreign political refugees. The entire Europe was teeming with American and Russian troops and hence ruled out for Bose.

Russia was the only country which could be relied on under the circumstances. According to the calculations of Netaji Bose, America and Russia were heading for a cold war after standing off over east and west Berlin, after the surrender of Germany in May 1945. Bose also realized that with the dropping of the atom bomb over Japan, the Americans were trying to dominate the Russians in Europe. Bose realized that Russian dictator Stalin would welcome a political leader like him from India, just to keep the British and Americans at bay in south Asia. Moreover even though Bose had hobnobbed with Hitler, an arch enemy of Russia, Stalin would be aware that Bose had done this purely for securing freedom for his motherland. Bose had a personal fascination for the Soviet Union as he liked their communist style of governance, where equality was maintained among the masses. Coming from a socialist school of thought, Bose found that the Soviet Union had the best system of governance as compared to the capitalist system adopted by America and her west European allies. This naturally endeared himself to old Russia and he was determined to seek asylum in the Soviet union under her dictator Joseph Stalin.

Meanwhile the Japanese Army high command was very concerned about the safety of Netaji Bose and requested him to suggest how he would like to rehabilitate himself after the surrender to Britain and America. It was an open secret that the Japanese high command had great respect for Bose not only as a military commander but also as an intellectual par excellence. Most of the higher level Japanese military officers were of the Samurai clan who admired bravery and sacrifice. They had studied the profile of Bose before and after he took command of the INA in Singapore and found him to be top drawer stuff. They loved the way he always led from the front and how firmly he dealt with his INA officers and soldiers. There was a mixture of love, compassion and strategy that he used to build up the INA as a fighting fit force in South East Asia. As a result of his activities the Japanese were very concerned that Netaji Bose should escape the clutches of the British and American invading forces in Asia.

There was a detailed field meeting held with the local Japanese army officers in Singapore on how best to have an exit plan for Bose. Various options were discussed including outright surrender, but this was rejected since the allies would certainly eliminate Bose at the earliest instant. They would use the Lookout Notice that had been in circulation all over the world across the British empire to take him prisoner, dead or alive! Hence it was imperative that Bose leave South East Asia immediately.

After protracted discussions, it was agreed that going to the Soviet Union would be the best possible option for Bose. Now the route map had to be finalized, keeping in mind de-militarized routes to the Soviet Union. There was no way that Bose could fly to Moscow directly without getting the permission of Joseph Stalin. Since the surrender had already been made, there was no way anybody could directly cross the border into Russia. Hence the closest land border with Russia had to be negotiated first. The most obvious way of approaching Soviet Russia from Asia was most certainly the Manchurian border. And since the Japanese already had control of Manchuria it made it easy for Bose to travel there without fear of detection and capture. Moreover the Soviet border with Manchuria was along southern Siberia, which was not a heavily military patrolled area. Also with the surrender of Japan, the Japanese forces had mostly withdrawn from the Soviet border. This presented a golden route for Bose to seek asylum in Soviet Russia.

After due consultation with the Japanese High Command, Bose decided to fly to the closest border town of Dairen on the Manchurian border by a Japanese special flight which took off from Formosa, now called Taiwan. The small aircraft landed in a jungle airstrip specially created for it, very close to the Siberian border in Soviet Russia. The local Japanese army unit stationed on the Manchurian side had established communication with their Russian counterparts that a VIP politician from Asia was visiting Dairen and was seeking to meet their supreme commander Mr. Joseph Stalin. The response from the Soviet side was non-commital and Bose was taking a huge risk by traveling without a formal invitation. The Russians however did not deny him entry, either.

The Japanese aircraft landed in Dairen and waited at the airstrip for some time. Soon a Russian military jeep crossed over form the jungles adjoining the Siberian border and came up to the airstrip. There was a brief exchange of words between the Russian officers and the Japanese aircraft crew. Bose was transferred into the Russian jeep which drove him into the Siberian side of the Manchurian border. The aircraft took off immediately afterwards. From here onwards there has been no corroborated sightings of Bose and everything is in the realm of imagination. However, from the open press conference conducted by our popular MP, Dr. Subramaniam Swamy around 2016, the facts of what happened to Netaji Bose in Russia seems extremely tragic. It appears that Bose was taken into preventive custody by the local Siberian police outpost pending further orders from Moscow.

Even for people who are used to betrayal and lies, what is happening now was very scary to read. The news of Netaji Bose's entry into Russian territory itself is mired in controversy. Did Bose obtain prior permission from dictator Joseph Stalin before he took off from Taiwan? Or did he take a big leap of faith hoping that the local Soviet army or police units at the Siberian border would allow him entry even if it meant being under their custody? Whatever was the methodology of entry, it appears that Bose was kept in custody until the news of his identity was flashed to Stalin in Moscow. Based on his military intelligence inputs, Stalin realized that he was in possession one of the key members of India's freedom struggle. The one aspect that was bitter to swallow for Stalin was that Bose had actually had a closed door meeting with his arch enemy, Adolf Hitler, and a common enemy for the entire Allied forces. Much as Stalin would have loved to associate more closely with Bose, he realized he was sitting on a ticking time bomb.

Russian dictator Joseph Stalin was in a delimma on what to do with Bose, who was seeking asylum in his country. Stalin ordered all the information his intelligence bureau could garner on Bose and after perusing through them he realized he was dealing with a brilliant and popular statesman from India, somebody who was truly a revolutionary freedom hero in his country. However, he was in a deep quandary on how to deal with Bose's request for political asylum in Russia. On the one hand, Bose was a fugitive of the British government who wanted him dead or alive. Stalin did not for one moment forget that Britain was one of his allies in the second world war against Nazi Germany. On the other hand, Stalin had very poor trust over both his allies, Britain and America, given their ancient rivalries over territories in Asia and Europe. He realized that he could actually use the presence of Bose on his soil as a bargaining tool with both Britain and America.

There was one more angle that Stalin looked at on his appraisal of Bose. He did not take kindly to the fact that Bose had gone to Germany and dined with the devil himself. If there was one person that Stalin would never forgive it was Hitler, whom he considered a traitor for having invaded Russia in 1942 without provocation and breaching the mutual peace treaty agreement. Stalin was miffed that Bose had gone halfway round the world just to cohort with a monster in Germany. Being a revolutionary himself during his youth, Stalin did realize that Bose took a very tactical decision to align with Hitler just to get even with their common enemy, Britain. He must have also realized that at that point of time Germany was the only option open for military assistance for Bose. Yet it was galling for him to digest the fact that Bose had gone and befriended a megalomaniacal genocide perpetrator, who had raped Soviet Russia with his army and airforce.

Stalin had to take a hard decision sooner than later. He called the British PM, Winston Churchill, with the news of Bose in Russia. Churchill was apparently stunned but advised Stalin to keep this a secret for fear it would create a riot in India if the news reached there. Stalin was advised to do nothing until the news was conveyed to certain people in India. The certain people were certainly the Viceroy of British-India and the Queen's office. It is purported that news of Bose's internment in Soviet Russia also reached Nehru through the mouth of Mrs. Edwina Mountbatten. However there are two views on this. The other view is that the news was kept secret from all Indians and only transmitted to Nehru after independence, once his Prime Minister post was a confirmed formality. That secret was possibly shared by the next PM of Britain, Mr. Clement Atlee, after Winston Chruchill demitted office soon after the second World War in 1945. The end action of all those privy to this sensational incident, was to remain silent and do nothing. The British obviously wanted to keep this a secret because the immense popularity of the Netaji Bose would most certainly culminate in an uprising in India and put paid to Nehru becoming independent India's first PM. The British would any day be happy with Nehru as PM than an armed revolutionary like Netaji Bose.

Stalin very reluctantly decided to keep the presence of Bose in Russia a secret and use it as a bargaining chip at a later point in time. However the immediate task at hand was what to do with Bose. He may have been a national hero back in India, but in Russia he was still a foreign fugitive. While Bose remained in protective custody for a few days, Stalin decided to deal with him as a political prisoner. Hence he ordered bose to be dispatched to a remote Siberian prison for detention.

When Nehru received the news that Bose was indeed in Russia, he was at first shocked, then he broke out into cold sweat. Here was his arch-rival and old party colleague who had obviously come back to life after the story of his death in a plane crash in August 1945. The first thought that ran through Nehru's mind was to protect his Prime Ministers chair at any cost. He knew that if there was one person in India who could take over his PM throne it was only Netaji Bose. The moment he dreaded had arrived. A direct threat to his leadership from his former Congress Party colleague was currently alive. The news of the plane crash and death of Bose was a great relief for quite a few "Gandhians" in the Congress party, including Gandhi himself. Unknown to many, both Indians and foreigners, the plane crash story was a bluff circulated by the Japanese government to create a smoke screen for his escape into Manchuria. Only people close to Bose knew that many Japanese in both their government and army actually admired and respected Netaji Bose for his intellect and humanity. He was a big hit in Japan and Germany. Wherever he went, he commanded respect for the way he carried himself and spoke with strong common sense and wide knowledge.

Nehru decided to play it safe. He kept this news tightly locked up in his chest and through diplomatic channels in the British government, requested the

British PM to keep this news secret. After Nehru became the first PM of India, he had the option of releasing Bose from the Russian prison and bringing him back to India as a war hero. However the extremely jealous nature of this so-called statesman prevented him from executing this humane step to help a fallen comrade. Nehru was in very close touch with British PM, Clement Attlee and both had a tacit understanding to keep news of bose in Russia a top secret. It appears India's Vice-President, Dr. Radhakrishnan also had an inkling that Bose was interred in Russia and he did actively tried to probe more details during his official visits to Russia. On some occasions, it appears Nehru got wind of his activities and adviced him against probing such details.

Now comes the one billion dollar question, if Nehru was aware that Bose was indeed in Russia and did nothing about it, was he not guilty of murder? According to the Press Conference that noted BJP MP, Mr. Subramaniam Swamy, gave a few years ago and we were lucky to witness on video, he made a very categorical assertion that Nehru did in fact know of the imprisonment of Bose and he did nothing about it. Swamy further goes on to tell us that Bose continued in the Siberian prison till the mid-1950s till his premature death due to the extreme cold and solitary confinement. His body was thrown into the icy Siberian wasteland without a proper burial. History records that dictator Stalin died in 1953. The question in everybody's mind is whether Stalin understood the gravity of imprisoning a freedom hero of India or whether he kept tabs on Bose in prison, at least to monitor his health. After the death of Stalin, it is extremely possible that the succeeding president of Soviet Russia was not apprised of the fact that Bose was in a remote Siberian prison. It is possible that this lack of information led to the neglect of Bose in prison and he died of a broken heart.

What is the reason that successive governments of India have refused to delve into the exact cause of the death of Bose? Why is that when the Taiwan plane crash theory was debunked by the Mukerjee Commission due to total lack of concrete evidence, that none of the central governments, including the present BJP, is not willing to investigate further? Is the fear of spoiling relationship with countries like Russia that is keeping even an non-Congress PM like Mr. Narendra Modi from investigating further? Is the strategic relationship with a military power like Russia more important that getting to the truth of the actual death of our own freedom hero? Is there a role of some other party or organization behind the imprisonment and the death of Bose in a Russian prison? Who is the government of India trying to protect by refusing to declassify the remaining few Netaji Files.

Why is the only daughter of Netaji Bose, Dr. Anita Bose, not making an official request for a DNA analysis of her father's ashes that presently lie in Renkoji temple in Tokyo? Even though she is not convinced with the Taiwan air-crash theory, she is not asking for details on the Russian imprisonment of her father. Why is there no public outcry on the absolute lack of concrete information on the actual death of Netaji Bose? Has the Indian public become so used to hearing conflicting information on Bose over the last 70 years, that they simply don't care anymore? Or is this sheer ingratitude of our public to one of the founding pillars of our freedom movement?

# 16. The Red Fort Trials

After the end of the second world war in August 1945, the British deported the INA troops back to India to face trial and punishment. While the soldiers were kept in confined barraamcks under guard, the INA officers were put on trial. Among the famous officers of the INA, three of them were selected to be role models to suffer punishment, including execution by hanging. The three INA officers selected to stand trial at the Red Fort in Delhi on the charges of waging war against the British empire were Col. Dhillon, Col. Sehgal and Col. Shah Nawaz Khan. The trials were slated for November 1945 and the news was made public, so that other Indians would be dissuaded to take part in any anti-British activities in future.

What the British government in India hoped to give a moral lesson to Indian citizens turned around to become a nightmare for them. The Red Fort trials incensed the patriotic feelings of the entire country and what was slated to be a cake-walk for the British, turned out to become their greatest disaster. News began to spread far and wide across the country that INA officers who had risked their lives abroad for India's freedom were being put to death. What the British had achieved by doing a news black-out of the INA during the second world war days was torn asunder by the outpouring of human indignation at seeing one of their own patriotic fellow countrymen being sent to the gallows.

Sensing the mood of the general public, Gandhi called for total support for the under-trial INA officers. He even requested Nehru to lead the panel of lawyers to plead the case of the INA officers against the British Raj. It was a classic case of crass opportunism that Gandhi, who until then had disdained both Netaji Bose and his INA troops, was now openly rooting for the protection of these very same INA officers. Even Nehru who was openly sarcastic about the INA was seen in his advocate attire and rushing to the trials in the Red Fort. The irony of the whole issue was not lost on some truly open minded freedom fighters like Dr. Ambedkar and Sardar Patel. The public must have wondered at the sudden change of heart of the Congress leaders but the gravity of the matter probably overrode the change in principles of the fired up Congress party. One should not forget it was the same Gamdhi exactly one decade ago, who refused to intervene on the death sentence given to our immortal freedom hero, Shaheed Bhaghat Singh. Gandhi refused to challenge the order of the British Raj sentencing Bhaghat Singh to hang in Lahore central prison, even when he knew that his words would turn the sentence aside with his mass appeal among the Indian public. The British feared Gandhi's power of Satyagraha but this time Gandhi was unwilling to use his Brahmastra to save the life of young Bhaghat Singh.

Actually, the real reason for the change in mind of Gandhi and the Congress was pure arithmetics. The Congress Party in 1945 had nothing going popular for them during and after the second world war. The last major national event that had been conducted was the Quit India Movement of 1942. However since the war in Europe was still going on, Gandhi had two minds about supporting the war against Nazi Germany and internally felt that Indians should morally support Britain against the fascists. Hence the Quit India Movement did not have much steam in its popularity with the masses. Due to the British preoccupation with the second world war, there was no adverse reaction by the local police to the Quit India Movement. It is not wrong to say that the Quit India Movement was a partial failure and the steam of the freedom movement was greatly reduced during the second world war years. Thus when the war ended in august 1945, there was hardly any resistance being shown by either the masses or the freedom fighter of the Congress party. Hence when the INA trials began in October 1945, it acted as a catalyst for mass unrest and civil disobedience, which even galvanized the Congress Party leaders. The shrewd political mind that Gandhi was, he seized this golden opportunity to revive the sagging fortunes of the Congress Party fighting for freedom.

The Red Fort trials which began in great fanfare by the British Raj in India hoping for an early verdict to hang the three INA officers, now ran into rough weather, with violent protests breaking out in streets all over India. The entire nation burst into flames, galvanized by the memory of Netaji Subash Chandra Bose and how much he had sacrificed his life for the freedom struggle of India. The mere fact that Bose had disappeared from public view in mid-August did not deter the protestors in putting their full support against the trials. As the protests spread from the larger cities like Bombay, Delhi, Calcutta and Madras to the smaller towns all over India, it became clear to the British that they had opened up a Pandora's box. Even as the public demonstrations began to snowball into a national movement, the British hastily backtracked on their charges of sedition and instead changed the charges into a case of military desertion by the INA officers from the royal British army.

Meanwhile the Congress Party leaders donned their lawyer costumes and made a huge show of supporting the accused INA officers legally. The irony of the whole incident was not lost on the educated public of India. Here were some INA officers who were part of the establishment of Netaji Bose and the very same Congress Party which had decried Bose and called him an apostate when he contested the Congress president post against the candidature of Gandhi's disciple, was now bending backwards to protect the INA officers. The entire drama reeked of hypocrisy of the highest order and was orchestrated by the father of the nation ,himself. The whole world watched as Gandhi suddenly decided that the INA was not that really a bad organization and that certain patriotic Indians had been mesmerized to joining the same. The about turn in such an attitude was not lost on many historians, including British ones, who have openly castigated Gandhi for being a crass opportunist in such a national crisis.

Not only was Gandhi and the Congress able to take maximum mileage from the Red Fort trials, they also managed to turn the tables on the British Raj by reviving the sagging spirit of the freedom struggle that had gone into sleep mode during the second world war period in the early 1940s. The Red Fort trials represented a golden opportunity for the Congress Party to ride piggyback on the exploits of the INA so carefully crafted by Netaji Bose for over a decade of painstaking planning and logisitics. Within a week, the Congress Party revitalized its organizational set up and harnessed the nation wide agitation to their absolute advantage. This was free publicity for the Congress Party at work, using the sweat and toil of the INA, whom Gandhi and the Congress had disdained not too long ago as being a violent freedom army.

The British called off the trials and decided just to try the INA officers for petty desertion. On the insistence of Gandhi, the INA officers were finally exonerated of all crimes. The British bluff to seal the fate of the INA officers and make it a model code of conduct for all INA detainees backfired and were made to face the bitter reality that the INA had actually succeeded in firing the sleeping patriotism among the common Indian citizens. The British was made to finally acknowledge that even in military defeat, the INA had a huge part to play in the final surge for freedom. The Naval Mutiny that immediately followed the Red Fort trials is a standing testimony that the INA had instilled a deep sense of patriotism among the masses that even Gandhi in his heydeys could never hope to have achieved. The Red Fort trials will long be remembered as a moment of Indian identity against the hegemony and imperial torture of the hated British army and police in India. The Red Fort trials is a standing testimony of the resilience of the Indian public, regardless of the mesmeric charms of the Apostle of Peace, that was supposed to signify Ahimsaa, an intangible dream for independence of any nation.

# 17. The Naval Mutiny 1946

One of the direct consequences of the Red Fort trials was its incitement of the royal navy mutiny within a few months. The Royal Indian navy based in India basically consisted of British commissioned naval officers commanding Indian sailors and petty officers. No history of the Indian freedom struggle is complete without the detailed mention of the Naval Mutiny or in a more veiled parlance Naval Uprising. This mutiny that began in Bombay harbour found its way to the ports of Karachi, Visakapatnam, Madras, Calcutta and Cochin. This mutiny would have led to a major revolution and a blood bath against the British troops and police, if only the Congress Party had stood behind the mutineers.

The Naval Mutiny fizzled out mainly because the Indian National Congress (INC) as well its rival political party, the Muslim League refused to endorse the mutiny. Only the Communist Party of India (CPI) stood rock solid behind the naval and airforce ratings who conduted the mutiny. The stand taken by the INC was that since the British were anyway going to grant independence to India very shortly, there was no point in going for a revolution that could be couter-productive to the progress that the Congress aprreared to have made thus far. The Muslim League (ML) also was of the same opinion, since they were also in a terrible hurry to grab an independent Pakistan at the earliest. They were very clear that any untoward incident before the formal transfer of power by the British would ruin their chances of a smooth transfer of power for an independent Pakistan. While this was the official tack of both these leading political parties of undivided India at that time, the real reasons were actually selfish and sinister.

The real reasons for both the political parties refusing to support the Naval Mutiny has been explained very nicely by astute and neutral historians, both Indian and foreign. According to them, the INC and the ML were secretly scared that this rare show of public unity against the British occupying forces would actually result in Hindus and Muslims unifying for the common cause of independence and actually demand freedom for an undivided India. While on the one hand both the INC and the ML wanted a speedy transition of power, they were actually very scared that the mutiny would actually unite Hindus and Muslims, which would result in freedom for an undivided India.

Gandhi refused to endorse the naval agitation, claiming it was a violent struggle in direct contrast to his non-violent principles of Ahimsa. But it appears Gandhi was actually worried that his protégé, Nehru, would miss out being the Prime Minister of an independent India. Nehru had the same feelings since he was very clear that he was always the first choice Prime Minister of independent India. Sardar Patel supported them, since he did not want to stick out like a sore thumb in the party. But both Gandhi and Nehru had another secret grouse against the Naval uprising. They were absolutely alarmed that this uprising was actually instigated by the Death Sentences to be handed over to the three INA officers of Netaji Bose after the Red Fort trials. Both Gandhi and Nehru were secretly jealous of the mass popularity of Netaji Bose in India and abroad. They felt if they supported the Naval Uprising, the INA Officers would become very famous and could even stand for election at a future date. Moreover they were against giving any further publicity to the INA, which had already found a place in the hearts of most patriotic Indians. It was becomely abundantly clear to both Gandhi and Nehru that it was the INA that had turned the fortunes of the Indian freedom movement in the 1940s with their self-defence stance ,rather than the much vaunted Ahimsa of the Congress team.

The hero of the entire naval mutiny was the CPI that totally backed the agitators and were hoping of uniting the Hindu-Muslim factions in both the party and in general across the country to secure independence from the British. The CPI organized dharnas and mass civil disobedience across all the major port cities of undivided India during the entire period of the sepoy mutiny. The Naval Uprising proved that India could still unite, without getting bogged down with the common issues like religion, caste and language. It was a spontaneous reaction against the cruel practices of the British Raj which united both the sailors and the common public like never before.

The real provocation for the naval mutiny was actually the very slow pace of Demobilisation of the British Indian armed forces. Soon after the end of the second world war, the Indian sailors and airmen who returned back to India from Europe and Africa, were not allowed to return back home until further notice. The British took their own time to disband these returned troops and most of them remained idling in their respective barracks across the length and breath of

India. They had not seen their families for many years abroad and were yearning to meet them. Yet their British superiors were unwilling to diband them. The second grouse of these Indian sailors was that the food being provided in their barracks and ships were of sub-standard quality.

Bombay and Karachi ports were the two main centers of the naval uprising. While Bombay went off very well, it was Karachi harbour that gave us the maximum openings. The Karachi harbour was accessible from Keamari Naval district as well as the nearby Manora Island. The naval ratings captured the main naval destroyer parked in the harbour and trained its guns on the mainland facing the British army that was ordered to contain the revolt. However the lack of moral support from the INC and the ML resulted in the revolt fizzling out since the mutineers were scared to take the risk all alone, without political patronage. The INC persuaded the upper management of the strike committee to call off the strike, promising that the British Government would not punish the striking naval ratings. This promise was given with an unwritten understanding with the British government that there would be no recriminations after the strike was called off.

But to the horror of the Indian public, these very same naval ratings were put in prison and many were terminated from the Navy. To add to their misery none of these war experienced navy personnel were inducted either into the Indian navy or the Pakistan navy, immediately after partition. Quite obviously the INC and the ML would have signed a deal with the British Raj, that unless this clause was agreed upon, partition would have been delayed. The same fate awaited the soldiers and officers of the INA who were not inducted into the Indian army. However Pakistan, sensing the rich experience of the disbanded INA troops living in Pakistan, immediately inducted them into the Pakistan army for the 1947 Kashmir Operations against India. Many historians are of the view that one of the reasons why Pakistan was able to penetrate deep into Kashmir was the rich experience of the battle-hardened INA officers and soldiers, who easily swept through the weak resistance of the Kashmir Maharaja's ill equipped troops. The years of Guerilla war experience of these INA troops in the jungles of Burma and Malaya, worked to the advantage of the Pakistan army. Due to Nenru's stubbornness not to induct even a single INA soldier into the Indian army, we lost out on war strategy which would have otherwise played a great part in our intended victory.

Special mention should be made of the battle ship INHS Shamsher at the Bombay harbour, which refused to join the uprising just because it commanding officer Lt,Krishnan, a South Indian naval officer who decided to stay on with the British, inspite of his deputy officer, sub-Lt. Gandhi who wanted him to join the strike. Krishnan was able to convince his local sailors with an bombastic speech where he touched upon his Indian identity. He cajoled his sailors to take the ship out of the Bombay harbour and avoid the strike. Here we see a classic case of why the Indian independence struggle failed for the last 200 years. Time and again our freedom heroes were let down by traitors who let down the freedom struggle at opportune moments. Whether it was Jhansi Rani or Tippu Sulthan, there was always a Jai Chand to let down a brave Pritviraj Chauhan. Many historians find that turn-coats were common in the Indian independence sruggle and were one of the root causes of many agitations sizzling out in the long run, thereby delaying our ultimate independence by many decades.

All in all, the Naval Mutiny was a turning point in India's struggle for independence. In effect, it broke the back of the mighty British empire in India, whose claim that the sun never set on them was destroyed in one fell swoop. The infallibility of the British army and the royal navy lay in shambles at the end of the Naval mutiny. The British realized that the Point of No Return had finally come to them. They could no longer trust the local Indians employed as soldiers and officers in the British-Indian army, navy and airforce. This point was driven home by the ex-PM of Britain, Clement Atlee, who visited India immediately after he demited high office in 1950. On a visit to Calcutta, he met the chief justice of the Calcutta high court and had discussions with him in the Governor Bungalow. The Chief Justice asked him why the British left India so suddenly in 1947, when they could have taken a few more years to withdraw. The answer that Atlee gave is the same fact that is being repeated by many historians on India till date. Atlee mentioned that the British left India when they realized they had lost the trust of the British-Indian soldiers and officers stationed in India. This he attributed openly to the Subash Chandra Bose Effect caused by the INA Trials. He also reiterated that Gandhi was not the real cause of quitting India, it was Netaji Bose that contributed finally to the exit of the British from India.

# 18. Freedom with Partition

One of the most tragic instances in world history is the Partition of India. Many of us have heard of the partion of Germany and Korea, but the partition of the Indian subcontinent was one of the most cruelest stroke by the British empire. India was certainly the brightest jewel in the British empire that had covered many parts of the world. After close to 300 years of subjugation, the British found it painful to leave. And the parting gift they gave us was the partition. However the way the way they went about this task was certainly cheap and dastardly. The British simply pitted the Muslims and Hindus of India against one another by deliberately creating rifts and animosity that ultimately went into public mob violence. Even a stalwart leader like Gandhi who professed to be secular and peace loving could not keep the monster of communalism at bay. It was a sad commentary that a foreign power from Europe played dirty politics to divide a nation which they had united in the first place.

The reason behind why Britain played dirty was the sense of anger of being kicked out of a subcontinent they had subjugated for over three centuries. In their opinion, India was a deeply divided land when they first set foot on, broken up into many scores of small kingdoms. It was the British which consolidated all these small kingdoms and integrated the territories into one homogenous country called India. The British certainly brought in much needed political, economic and educational reforms. They certainly did up the complete infrastructure of the country linking it with roads, bridges, dams and canals. Their buildings were strong and sturdy and stood the test of time and weather. They built up the educational and health system also, bringing scientific temper into an otherwise superstitious way of life. Having done up all this networking the British felt they had to play spoil-sport before they handed over all this infrastructure back to Indian hands.

The partition of India was hastened by the presence of two radical political parties in the system. The Congress Party was the largest party dominating the landscape with a secular agenda, but the other two parties had other agendas.

One was the RSS and the other the Muslim League. Both parties were rooting for their respective religions alone, one for the Hindus and the other for the Muslims of India. While both claimed support from their respective religious followers, there was a sizeable chunk of people in India, who were truly secular and rooted for the Congress Party alone.

The RSS or the Rashtriya Sevak Sangh comprised of hard core Hindutva followers who believed that India must become an independent Hindu nation alone and stood by the concept of the partition of India, into a Hindu India and a Muslim Pakistan. They were lead by their ideologue and Marathi crusader, Mr. Savarkar, who was hell bent on creating a Hindu Rashtra. On the other side of the communal spectrum was Mr. Mohammed Ali Jinnah, a progressive minded, London-educated Muslim, who was pushed into communal politics after seeing the antics of the RSS. Till the formation of the Muslim league, Jinnah was just an ordinary leader of the Congress party. During some of the early meetings, he found the behavious of both Gandhi and Nehru to be condescending and sometimes patronizingly arrogant. As the British brought him under their influenze, Jinnah began to root for a separate Muslim country called Pakistan. The Muslim league party seemed a perfect home for him and because of his sophisticated and western outlook to life, he turned out to be the natural leader of the Muslim masses of India, who were chafing under the Hindutva domination of the RSS.

In contrast to these bipolar views were both Netaji Bose and Dr. Ambedkar, who believed in an undivided ,independent India. Dr. Ambedkar was the undisputed natonal leader of the lower castes of India, particularly the Dalits and the tribal villagers. Educated abroad in Columbia University, USA, Ambedkar was focused on the task at hand which was to emancipate the lower fringes of society which included the Schedulaed Castes and Tribes of India. He drew inspiration from legendary, former president of America, Mr. Abraham Lincoln. As a strong crusader for the under-previledged in society, Ambedkar often clashed with Gandhi over the speed of implementation of schemes to uplift the downtrodden in India. He maintained that Gandhi was far too slow in implementating welfare measures, for which the British Government was willing to carry forward. Gandhi on the other hand was finding it difficult to balance Ambedkar against the other senior Congress leaders, particularly Nehru and Sardar Patel. It was to Dr. Ambedkar's credit that he never fought for a separate land for his sizeable Dalit and tribal followers.

Netaji Bose refused to entertain any thoughts of partitioning India, calling the concept a deliberately diabolical move by the British to divide and rule the Indian people. Netaji lived and breathed secularism hence it was anathema to him to even think of dividing the subcontinent into a separate Hindustan and Pakistan. Even while in India when the concept of the two nation theory came into usage around the mid-1930s ,Bose made his disgust very clear. He met and cautioned both Savarkar and Jinnah on the evils of dividing our nation into two separate countries based on religion alone. Neither of them gave him any positive replies at that point of time. When Bose left India secretly in early 1941, he was desperately trying to stop the impending partition of India, which he felt both Gandhi and Nehru were secretly espousing, even though they seemed against the call for Pakistan by Jinnah. Even after reaching Europe and later Japan, Netaji gave very strong speeches in all the foreign parliaments and public meetings, condemning the concept of partition. Even in his radio broadcasts in both Radio Japan and Radio Berlin in the 1940s, Netaji warned all Indians against supporting the call for partition. He warned of the twin dangers of religious communalism and separatism. He requested all Indian citizens to be vigilant against the divide and rule tactics of the British Raj.

It appeared the main supporter of partition was Mohammed Ali Jinnah with the British secretly backing him with everything in their means. It very much appeared that the British were creating a mess for the Indian sub-continent, before they quit it for good. They were very well aware of the repercussions of partition, even if the dangers of the same were not truly understood by the Muslim League or by the Hindu Mahasabha. The British very well knew there was every possibility of a blood-bath since it involved loss of homes and property on both sides of the divide. It was truly a catastrophe in the making and it was imperative that the Congress Party did their best to prevent the impending partition.

It is still a huge mystery why Gandhi finally succumbed to the majority decision to go ahead with the tragic portion of India. With the whole country and indeed the rest of the civilized world looking on,why did the Father of the Nation go ahead with the majority decision to take the fatal plunge of dividing the sub-continent? Why was a man who believed totally in the unity of both Hindus and Muslims to live together in harmony, take such an earth-shattering decision which cost roughly one million human lives on both sides of the political and religious divide? Why did the Apostle of Peace be lulled into allowing the tragic partition of India, when he knew very well the immense impending family sacrifices, and financial anguish on both sides of the religious divide? How could a popular man like Gandhi with such a mass following, actually assume that partition was inevitable and we had to swallow that bitter pill, come hell or high water? How could a person who revered non-violence as a way of life actually fall into the trap of giving the green signal for all hell to break loose in the form of cross-border civil violence and mass upheaval?

The answer to all the above questions is there to deduce but extremely painful to swallow. Gandhi threw up his hands for two solid reasons. One, the Hindu-Muslim situation in the mid-1940s had more or less hardened with the two major stake holders supporting the partition of the sub-continent, namely the Hindu Mahasabha and the Muslim League. The Congress officially objected to partition due to the public stand taken by Gandhi, but prominent Hindu leaders within the Congress began to secretly support partition since they found the stringent stand of the Muslim League too harsh. The Muslim leaders within the Congress did not want partition. Among the Hindu leaders, Nehru stood out for his intent to go ahead with partition for purely selfish reasons. He was dead set on becoming the first Prime Minister of India and Jinnah had openly challenged his monopoly to the PM chair. By dividing India into two, Nehru wanted to stake his post as the first PM of Hindu India.

The second reason for Gandhi to agree for partition was his promise to Motilal Nehru to make his son, Jawaharlal, the first PM of independent India. Unfortunely the father of the nation had his favourites and Nehru was with his first among all equals. With the passage of time it became obvious to Gandhi that he had lost his grip on the Muslim masses since Jinnah had slowly taken over as the messiah of the Indian Muslims. Unfortunately Gandhi was not the invincible leader of India as many historians would have us believe. He had his eccentricities and his fallacies which was not palatable to many people, including Mohammed Ali Jinnah. Moreover Jinnah's demand to become undivided India's first PM didi not go down well with the Congress leaders. Gandhi was willing to consider this demand, but he was met with long faces within the Congress, many of whom did not trust Jinnah. Nehru steadfastedly refused to budge from his intent to become the first Prime Minister of independent India.

Many historians often ask that one billion dollar question on why Gandhi did not resort to the only weapon that used to work on the Indian masses to prevent the partition, namely the Hunger Strike Sathyagraha? When Gandhi could stop the communal violence in Bengal with his Sathyagraha, why didn't he use this technique to prevent a dangerous monster like the partition? Is it because he realized that the Congress had not done enough to address the concerns of the minorities and down-trodden people of India? Was he worried that he would not get the required mass support against partition if he sat on an indefinite hunger strike? Why did the Apostle of Peace falter when it mattered most? Had he already given up his hold on the Indian Muslim masses due to the huge popularity of the Muslim League and Jinnah? Did he feel his name would be tarnished if the masses refused to heed his hunger strike Satyagraha and he would lose his respect as the Father of the Nation? Did he also feel that even the Dalits and the downtrodden lower castes of India would ignore him since he did not have the best of relations with their undisputed leader, Dr. Ambedkar?

The end result was that Gandhi vacillated at that critical junction before the actual partition of India, which cost us a million human lives, apart from physical violence, rape and millions of rupees worth of property damages. Obviously the Congress Party had not done their homework well enough to estimate the huge cost of partition, both in human and material terms. In his hunger for power and position, Nehru goaded Gandhi to go ahead with partition, as if that was the only option. With both the secular pillars of India's freedom struggle like Netaji Bose and Dr. Ambedkar firmly against the partition of India, the Congress Party took a gamble that turned out to be a nightmare for the entire sub-continent. The result was unmitigated violence, rape and property damage on both sides of the new border. People were butchered in broad daylight, women were mercilessly raped and children became orphans overnight as entire localities were set on fire by armed mobs roaming the streets unchecked. The myth of a peaceful settlement between the newly formed Pakistan and the Indian state vanished into thin air, the moment the clarion call for partition was sounded. What started out as mob violence later led to permanent rivalry between the two countries which would continue to bleed the two nations in a costly war of attrition that continues to be the cynosure of all eyes on this planet. Today the two nations have gone to war four times costing both nations a huge cost in human lives and property, not to mention needless expenditure in armaments when that same funds could go to feeding the teeming, poverty-stricken masses on both sides.

The partition of India itself was an exercise in futility and reeked of grave errors in geo-political terms. Pakistan was created keeping in mind territories that had higher concentrations of Muslims to Hindus. To that extent, the large states of Punjab and Bengal had to be broken up. Western Punjab went to Pakistan while India got eastern Punjab. West Bengal cam to India while East Bengal went to Pakistan. Both these states were highly agricultural states. Punjab was the wheat basket of old Hindustan, while Bengal was the rice basket of old Hindustan. The Indus river along with 5 other rivers irrigated Punjab, while the Gangetic Delta was home to Bengal. Both were highly populated states and the disruption of partition was bound to bring massive upheaval in both the states. And that's exactly what happened when partition began. Rivers of blood flowed through both Punjab and Bengal, during those critical days and months following the partition of the India. Gory scenes of mass burning, executions, rape and arson were reported on a daily basis and the world watched as the entire subcontinent exploded into one big mass of blood and hatred.

Overnight friendly neighbourhoods became hostile and people attacked one another like animals. Women who were considered sisters till yesterday were raped in broad daylight, stripped naked and even had their private parts mutilated in public. A subcontinent that prided itself on giving the world a Sanathana Dharma like the peaceful Hindu religion, suddenly exploded into a frenzy and orgy of communal violence. The land of the Buddha was aflame with anger and revenge like no other time in its long history. India had boasted having hosted major and famous battles and wars in its five thousand year history, but this was one bloody Civil War that culminated in the death of one million human lives in the sub-continent. There can be hundreds of debates on how this national carnage could have been avoided, but it would finally boil down to the Father of the Nation Mr. Mohandas Karamchand Gandhi.

Generations of Indians and foreigners will continue to ask the one million dollar question.....Why was Gandhi not able to Unite the Country, If he was indeed the Real Father of the Nation? What prevented Gandhi on going on his traditional Hunger Strike to compel all Indians to rally under one flag, regardless of their religion,,caste and language. It indeed Gandhi loved that song *Raghupathi Raghava, Raja Ram Eeswhar, Allah, Tero Naam* then he would have made sure Hindus and Muslims would have united and fought for independence against the British, united in body and spirit. However history tells us that Gandhi could not sustain the pressure due to his soft corner for Nehru, whom he had sworn to make the first PM of India. History tells us that Gandhi could not envisage handing over the top chair of the country to a Muslim called Mohammed Ali Jinnah, even if that chair would be rotated between Jinnah and Nehru.

The partition helped the two super-powers, Russia and America, to make India and Pakistan their vassal states, simply by supplying them arms and ammunition on a continuous basis. It provided a golden opportunity to improve the economies of the two super-powers at the cost of these two warring nations. Hence the cold war extended its way into the Indian sub-continent, by the opportunity given by the partition. Both India and Pakistan became the laughing stocks of the world. Here were two impoverished nations battling it out with expensive weapons systems brought with precious money that could otherwise go to feeding their starving millions. The rivalry even resulted in a larger common neighbour taking undue advantage to boss around in the neighbourhood. The communist regime of China took advantage of India's military preoccupation with Pakistan, to gobble up an independent country called Tibet, having a long land border with India across the high Himalayas. As the Chinese red Army, entered the large, indepent country of Tibet and pushing south to the Indian border, Prime Minister Nehru refused to acknowledge the massive threat. Instead he mistakenly indulged in wishful dreaming, calling China a benign, big brother.

The big brother went ahead annexing Tibet in the early 1950s by using violence and armed force on the innocent Tibetan tribal people on this large, Himalayan plateau. Many monastaries, entire residential localities and farms were burnt down and people were imprisoned and made to do forced labour. The unique Tibetan language and culture was slowly but surely destroyed and made redundant in an atmosphere only conducive for the invading Han Chinese people. The destruction of Tibet was witnessed mutely by Nehru who never thought that the Chinese army would invade India across the high Himalayas. But on 20th October 1962, the Chinese red army simultaneiously crossed the Himalayas in Ladhakh and Arunachal Pradesh, on the western and eastern regions respectively, smashing the Indian army at various points across the international border with Tibet. They went on to occupy large parts of the Pangong lake basin in ladhakh and some parts around Arunachal Pradesh.

Even today India is sadly trapped between the hostile armies of Pakistan in the west and China in the north, across our large Himalayan Border. While the rest of the world talks of world peace and disarmament, India appears to have lost the track. With its teeming millions as the country with the largest population in the world, it is indeed a tragedy that even today one third of our population continues to remain below the poverty line. Hence, instead of spending precious resources to feed our millions, we are currently fittering it away into needless purchase of expensive arms and ammunition to counter both Pakistan and China. With the early Congress regime of first Nehru and then his daughter, Indira Gandhi, trying to make peace with Pakistan became an impossibility because of the belligerent stand of Pakistan towards the Kashmir border. Matters got worse when Pakistan teamed up with China across the Karakoram Border with Pakistan occupied Kashmir and actually ceded Kashmirir territory to China. The construction of the Karakoram Highway in the mid-1980s sealed the military and economic relations between Pakistan and China permanently. From then on the relations between these two enemy nations of India grew from strength to strength and has become a permanent nightmare for India and a constant drain on our vital resources. The Karakoram Highway became the economic corridor for China to access the Arabian sea via the Pakistani port of Karachi. Moreover this highway became the transit route for Chinese arms and missiles to reach Pakistan to be used against the Indian army. The worst nightmare for India across the Himalayas had come true.

## 19. An Ungrateful Nation

Due to the dominating British censorship in pre-independent India, news of Netaji Bose and the status of the INA was kept secret and what news finally leaked out was mostly unreliable. Sometimes news of Bose and the INA was actually twisted to give false information by the Congress Party and its cohorts. The alleged death of Netaji in an aircrash in Taiwan on August 18, 1945 was given utmost importance and flashed all over the national radio and newspapers across India. It was stunning news at that time which deeply shocked the nation. Most people believed this news of his death, but people very close to the INA in the fields of operation had their own doubts. For these battle-hardened officers and soldiers of the INA, who were aware of the geo-politics of the situation, they took the news rather cynically. Bose had survived many dangerous moments in his life during his quest for Indian independence and for him to die in an aircrash seemed too remote for many of his hardened fans. With the British Raj very much in India during 1945, there was nothing much to do but to accept the news.

After independence in 1947, the free press decided to do some investigation on its own. It was then that Japanese, British and American troops stationed in the vicinity of Taiwan confirmed that there was no aircrash during that fateful day of August 18, 1945. The statements of Netaji Bose's fellow air passenger, Col. Habib-Ur-Rahman did not seem to corroborate the actual crash theory. There was no military log entry in the Taihoku Air base where the crash allegedly happened. This air-crash was supposed to have taken the lives of senior Japanese army officers as well, but the Japanese military records did not seem to corroborate these events either. There were certain Japanese army officers and INA officers who swore that Netaji's flight was bound for Manchuria since he wanted to take political asylum in the Soviet Union, across the international border with old Manchuria.

However it was the Indian National Congress Party that indulged in the worst possible rumour mongering about Bose. In debate after debate, the

Congress made it very clear that Bose had indeed died in the air-crash and his ashes were interred in the Renkoji Temple at Tokyo. There were rumours that certain Indian diplomatic visitors to Soviet Union had private knowledge that Bose was locked up in a remote Siberian prison. Certain INA and Japanese army officers mentioned that the ashes of Bose kept in an urn in Renkoji Temple actually belonged to a Japanese soldier who had died on the same day in Taiwan. Rumours were flying thick and fast and the air-crash theory was beginning to sound hollow.

While public support for an independent enquiry was growing, the government of India under PM Nehru constituted the Shah Nawaz Commission to enquire into the death of Bose in the early 1950s, however nothing conclusive came of it since the terms and scope of reference of this enquiry commission were very limited. Indira Gandhi, bowing to popular demand as a PM, constituted the Khosla Commission to enquire into Netaji Bose's death in the early 1970s. This commission concluded that Netaji Bose had indeed died in the air-crash but could not produce concrete evidence to back their claim. Their claims were based on circumstantial evidences which could not be corroborated. Finally it was left to a non-Congress government under PM Atal Bihari Vajpayee who constituted the Mukherjee Commission in the late 1990s which did a full scale investigation into the death of Bose. Justice Mukherjee himself travelled all the way to Taiwan and conducted the investigations himself along with his legal team. From the extensive interviews and records perused by this team, it became very clear to the commission that no such air-crash had occurred anywhere in Taiwan on that fateful day of August 18, 1945. No such crash had occurred anywhere in Taiwan few days before or after that fateful day. All the log books of the air base, airport authorities, historical archives, military and police records showed beyond doubt that no air accident had occurred on that fateful week.

With such overwhelming evidence that the air-crash theory was a big fake, why didn't successive Indian Governments try to go after the raw truth on the death of Netaji Bose? With such a large population in India still enthralled by the exploits and life history of Netaji Bose even after so many decades after his dissappearance, why didn't successive Congress and Non-Congress Central Governments not get to the ultimate truth of his death? What prevented the Congress from getting at the raw truth with so many government agencies at their disposal in the last few decades? We can understand both Nehru and Indira Gandhi being reluctant to get to the bottom of the Netaji mystery, since they had everything to fear about Bose. But why didn't the Vajpayee BJP government do some real spade work to dig out the actual truth of the dissapperance of Netaji Bose from the face of this earth? It is true that Mr. Vajpayee was the only Prime Minister of India till date who actually visited the Renkoji temple near Tokyo to pay respects to the ashes of Bose kept in the temple. However he wasn't able to make any headway to trace the trail and actual death of Netaji Bose.

So are we to conclude that India of today comprises of purely ungrateful people who are enjoying the fruits of the freedom earned by our freedom fighters with blood, sweat and tears? Why is that only popular politicians like Gandhi, Nehru, Indira Gandhi, Rajiv Gandhi, etc, have large monuments dedicated to them in the national capital, Delhi? How is that all these big people have a death memorial in the center of Delhi city, whereas one of the pillars of the freedom struggle like Bose does not have an independent monument? Why is that all these mentioned people have a birth- day and death day, whereas a mass movement national leader like Subash Bose simply does not have a death day? It sounds ridiculous that a country of one billion plus people cannot come out with a solution for the "mystery" of the disappearance of their national hero, Shri Netaji Bose. Surely there are people alive even today in India and abroad, who know or have the capacity to get behind the truth of the actual death of Bose. Why are these people silent or why is the successive central governments of India for the last 75 years after independence not making serious effort to get behind the truth of a freedom fighter par excellence? What is this Conspiracy Theory behind the massive cover-up of his death?

The aircraft crash theory was in effect a drama created by the Japanese to keep the whereabouts of Bose a secret from the prying eyes of the British and American intelligence agencies. The Japanese military top brass had deep respect for Netaji whom they often referred to as Bose San. Many of them actually considered him as an incarnate of the Buddha, such was his calm and composure even in hardships. His immense knowledge of world geo-politics and his high intellectual capacity was a major source of attraction to the Japanese military officers. The Japanese top brass truly believed that only Bose could help them expand their territories beyond India to west Asia. In all the meetings with their allies in Asia, the Japanese gave the utmost honour and respect to Netaji Bose, knowing very well that he was equally popular in South East Asia and Europe.

Why is that we hear of reports that Netaji Bose was sighted here and there in India in the disguise of a sadhu? By claiming that he was hiding in the deep jungles of central India, cheap politicians are actually making a mockery of this charismatic leader who gave his life blood for the freedom of India. The Congress Party on its part has gone out of the way to painting Bose as a terrorist who was hell bent on sabotaging the non-violent freedom struggle. It must be stated here that Bose went to prison as many times as Gandhi or Nehru did in the 1930s and early 1940s. Bose was often put in dangerous prisons like Mandalay in Burma, where only political exiles of the British empire were incarcerated. In fact, Bose lost one of his lungs after contracting tuberculosis disease from his cell in the Mandalay prison. Due to this the British were forced to send him home to India, fearing he would die in Burma which would create a massive riot in India. It was only due to his failing health that Bose was not sent to the dreaded Cellular Jail in the Andaman Islands, that would probably had put an end to his political career. The other main reason was that Bose was too popular a mass leader to be sent to Andamans and his dispatch to the cellular jail would have triggered a massive outbreak of mass demonstrations in the whole of India.

Bose's failing health forced the British to allow him to go to Europe to receive better medical treatment. This also made sure he wasn't around in India to create further trouble for the British rule in India. However this provided Bose a golden opportunity to develop contacts in Europe which he utilised to the hilt when he later escaped from India in early 1941 to build military ties with Germany. The famous meeting with Hitler in Berlin was a phenomenal move by Bose to cement the ties between India and Germany during the second world war. By meeting the top enemy of the British empire, Bose sent out a strong message that from then on he would leave no stone unturned in his quest for his nation's independence, the criticism levelled against him that he was meeting a war criminal who participated in the genocide of 6 million Jews can only be looked from hind-sight.

When Bose met Hitler, the news of atrocities against the Jews of Europe by the German government was only beginning. By the time bose left Europe for South East Asia, the full scale of the mass genocide was beginning to come out in the press. By this time Bose was dealing directly with the Japanese Army in Singapore. Bose was deeply disturbed by the military policies followed by Hitler in his invasion of Russia. He was very much in Germany, when Hitler launched Operaton Barbarosa, the military invasion of Russia on June 22nd, 1942. He was shocked by the decision since till then Russia was an ally of Germany, as the second world war advanced. Moreover, Bose was shocked at the sheer blunder of the decision of invading a huge nation that would be a heavy drain on Germany. Moreover, being a keen student of history and economics, Bose was aware that Hitler was commiting exactly the same mistake that emperor Napolean had committed a century ago, when France invaded Russia and paid a heavy price leading to its ultimate defeat. He was amazed that such an astute political leader like Hitler could actually take a plunge across the vast steppes of Russia endangering his troops in the ensuing winter months. And the Battle of Stalingrad in the winter of 1941 virtually broke the backbone of the German army.

The present central government, which professes to respect Netaji Bose, has a long way to go to resurrect the damage created by the previous Congress governments for the last fifty years. They can start the damage control by first releasing the balance Classified Files of Netaji Bose which will reveal that he actually died in a freezing, Siberian prison in Russia. They can then start the process of building a Permenant Memorial for Bose in Delhi, Calcutta and also Maduria in Tamil Nadu. The reason why the city of Madurai badly needs a Netaji Bose memorial is that it was the youth of Madurai region that flocked to Burma to join the INA from the shores of Tamil Nadu on hearing the clarion call of their iconic leader Shri Pon Muthu Rama Linga Devar. Netaji Bose has gone on record many times to register his gratitude to the people of Tamil Nadu, who had not just sent their youth from Tamil Nadu but actually contributed their youth also from the Indian labour colonies in Malaya and Burma. In fact, Netaji and Shri Thevar shared a very special relationship between them and indeed Bose received a lot of material help from Shri Thevar for the INA cause.

The present central government could also make good its promise to raise the status of Netaji Bose as the second pillar of Indias freedom movement, after Gandhi. The current government should start printing currency notes and other official media with the logo of Netaji Bose and his Indian National Army. This was a promise they made during the last elections but they are yet to make good their word. No central government university has yet been named after Bose, which is surprising since there are universities named after many freedom fighters. Yes, one island in the Andaman chain has been renamed after Bose, but that's just a drop of water in the vast ocean that "s India. We were promised that all our currency notes would have the photo of Bose, apart from the regular

Gandhi photos. We were also promised a huge memorial would be built for Netaji Bose close to Raj Ghat, where the body of Gandhi is presently interred. No new stadiums and government buildings have been recently named or renamed after Bose, which is not a good sign for a country that has institutionalised the names of Nehru, Indira and Rahul Gandhi.

In short, the respect and adulation due to one of the foremost and most adulated heroes of India's freedom struggle has not been forthcoming. We have been slow to acknowledge Bose's immense contribution to the final act of freedom in 1947. Even countries like Malaysia, Singapore, Vietnam, Indonesia and Burma have gladly acknowledged the role of Bose in bringing freedom to their respective countries from the yoke of British imperialism. Not only Indian residents of these countries, even locals from all walks of life gladly recollect how the INA marched through the streets of their towns enroute to the Indian border with Burma. They proudly remember the noble presence of Netaji Bose as he headed his convoy through the towns and villages of old Malaya and Burma, enroute to Manipur and Nagaland. Unlike armies of ruling coalitions, the INA was extremely disciplined and its soldiers never misbehaved with the local population even though they had the support of the ruling Japanese government. In fact, at every new village along the route to India, the INA was given a rousing welcome by the local people as the liberators of their nation under British imperialism. Netaji Bose himself was a picture of humility as he kindly requested the local people for financial and material donation, including food and clothes for his famished troops. The outpouring of money, gold and other material aid was huge and plentiful as the local people had real trust and faith in the soldiers and officers of the INA.

The worst crime that the people of India and successive central governments have bequeathed on Netaji Bose is by continuing to perpetrate the disinformation that Bose actually died in that imaginary 1945 plane crash in Taiwan. With overwhelming evidence to prove that the air crash never happened and that in high probability that Bose actually died in a Russian prison, there seems to be absolutely no pressure from the public for a final end to the "mystery" of his death. While the pressure continued to remain high in the 1990s and a few years later, currently it looks like either the Indian masses have got fed up with the suspense to how Bose actually died or simply resigned to the fate that no Indian Government would ever dare bell the cat of his death. Now close to 75 years have passed since Bose went missing from human civilization and yet India remains numb to the question that a final tombstone is required for each and every citizen of hers, especially the tombstone for one of her most daring and pouplar sons. While the press continues to rave and rant over Bose's whereabouts, the fact remains that Bose is no more alive, since its 125 years now from his birth day.

While a National Monument at Delhi to commomerate Netaji Bose is a must, a similar monument can come up in Calcutta, the city of his youth and subsequent adult life. Cuttack, the city of his birth, already has a museum dedicated to Bose. The only other city that can claim for a national monument for Netaji Bose would certainly be the city of Madurai in Tamil Nadu. Madurai was the city that saw much of its youth travelling from India to Burma simply to enlist in the INA in the early 1940s. These youth were inspired by the speeches of their local leader Shri Pon Muthu Ramalinga Thevar, who extolled the youth to follow Netaji Bose, who would eventually lead them to military victory against the British empire. The contribution of the Tamil people to the growth of the INA was epitomized in a nutshell by Netaji Bose in a speech he made in Burma during the jungle operations when he said "if I was to be born again, I would certainly wish that I would be born in the sacred land of our Tamil people who have contributed immensely to the growth of our INA."

The central government has recently built a large sized statue of Netaji Bose at the famous Raaj Path in new Delhi, which is certainly a positive development. However much more has to be done to keep the spirit of Bose and his doughty INA alive, so that future generations of Indians don't lose track of our historic freedom struggle. One of the Islands in the Andaman chain has also been renamed as Bose island, in memory of the historic landing of Netaji Bose in the Andaman Islands on December 30th, 1943, along with the Japanese Navy. There is also a race to upstage the achievements of Gandhi, the father of our nation, using Netaji Bose as an alternate vehicle. This is not in good taste, as our father of the nation certainly unified all Indians into one cohesive unit in his non-violent Ahimsaa struggle. His followers included Netaji Bose, Sardar Patel, Nehru and other Congress leaders who went on to become tall leaders in their own rights. So it is not right to compare the achievements of Gandhi versus Bose or anybody else. Each contributed cohesively to the ultimate objective, to attain Poorna Swaraaj from the imperial British government. Bose always respected Gandhi till the very end and had the highest regards for his leadership. However policy decisions led to the split in their paths when Bose decided that ahimsaa would not bring freedom for India. Hence the formation of the INA and the military collusion with Germany and Japan.

The current central government had promised to keep the photo of Netaji Bose in all currency notes, thereby giving him parallel status to Gandhi. However even after close to decade in power there is no sign of any Indian currency note with the photo of Bose. We were promised that public institutions and stadiums would be named after Bose, but nothing concrete has happened in the last one decade of the central rule in Delhi. We were promised that the true cause of the death of Bose would be investigated using the officially Classified Files of Bose which are available at the National Archives in Delhi. However even after close to a decade, we are no closer to the truth than we were under the Congress governments under Nehru or Indira Gandhi. In effect, nothing substantial has come of the election promises of the current central government, who has often declared that it was Netaji Bose who should have become the first Prime Minister of India. For a national party that has openly criticized both Nehru and Gandhi, this central government has remained toothless uptill date. That no major announcements or naming of government buildings and monuments in the name of either Netaji Bose or the INA was made in the last one decade surely indicates that there is something amiss in the central government in Delhi at the moment.

Has the current central government in Delhi back-tracked on their Netaji promises only because Netaji did not toe the line of the Hindu nationalists before independence? If indeed this is so, it is a sad commentary on a national level political party that has always insisted that it was only the Indian National Army under Bose which brought ultimate independence for India. We notice the photo of Bose in all the posters and flex boards of this party, during and outside of the election campaigns. If this party is giving so much of lip service to Bose, why is that they are not able to put to work any of their promises to retain the Bose legacy for India. This is then indeed hypocrisy on the part of the central government in not brining back the truth and rich history of Bose and his INA. How can a national political party holding the power of the central government refuse to uncover the dirty cover-up on Netaji Bose that has been going on for the last 60 long years? How can a party that claims that Bose is its true freedom hero afford to come up with lame excuses that certain "foreign powers" would be very upset if India was to unearth the dirty truth of Bose's untimely death? Is it more important for us as a truly democratic and secular nation to get at the truth behind our freedom fighter's death or is it more important that we appease certain world powers that hold the key to India's vital defence imports?

That again begs the question whether India does not have confidence in its own indigenous weapons developed by our DRDO scientists and we are interested only in importing our weapon systems from abroad at great cost.

These are questions that the Indian public should be asking its successive governments for the last 60 years. These are questions that raise the issue that India has become a country of ungrateful citizens who just don't care about their rich history and culture. It has perhaps become a country of business-minded baniyas, intent on only counting their income at the end of every measly day's work. It is increasingly becoming quite clear that the Indian public that was once so curious and eager to know about the whereabouts about their freedom fighters and their progeny, has now become so busy over their rich incomes and lifestyles, that they simply don't care about our country's golden past. The refusal of the government and the citizens of India to glorify the history of the INA is the first step for us to make another dangerous step towards another partition of India. By ignoring the glorious secular movement of the INA and its visionary leader like Netaji Bose ,India stands to repeat the blunder of the Hindu-Muslim animosity that created the partition of India 75 years ago. The recent mass violence and genocide in the border state of Manipur and communal clashes in a town in Haryana has started the alarm bells ringing, especially since it was in Manipur that the INA first entered sacred Indian soil and hoisted the free flag of India on April 14th, 1944.

It is also become increasingly clear that today there is a clear polarization of common people along religious lines for the last 10 years. The political climate across the country has contributed with people becoming more worried about their religion, caste and language than on real national development. The united nation that our Netaji Bose wanted to see is becoming more and more difficult to achieve due to political rhetoric by a section of the people who think that Hinduism should be the defining concept for a true Indian. They conveniently forget that it was a multi-religious and multi-cultural INA that brought freedom to our doorstep. Certain sections of our society are even casting aspersions on some famous freedom fighters of our nation, including Gandhi ji himself. While Gandhi had his limitations as the mass leader of our nation during the freedom struggle, he was the one who united all Indians under one banner against the British Raj. Even our first PM, Mr. Nehru, had his limitations but still went about with national development. Lets give him credit for that, even though he had only negative thoughts against Netaji Bose and the INA. It was unfortunate that the magnanimity that Netaji showed by naming one INA brigade as the Nehru Brigade, was not reciprocated by Nehru to the INA while he was PM for 17 long years.

# 20. The INA.......A Tamil Army?

With the whole world recognising the exploits of the Indian National Army as a major contributor for the freedom of India that came in 1947, it is indeed tragic that most Indians still think the INA was basically a North-Indian army. Nothing can be further from the truth, since the INA constituted more than 80% of its soldiers from Tamil origin. Only the officer ranks had a larger north Indian participation. In fact the language for communication in the INA rank and file was a combination of Hindi and Tamil. The reason for such a large population of Tamils was due to the fact that most of the Indian origin people staying in Burma, Malaya and Singapore were uneducated labour from the old Madras Presidency, today a combination of Tamil Nadu, Karnataka, Andhra Pradesh and Kerala. As a result, many of the labour colony parents were eager to give their sons and daughters for the cause of India's freedom. They allowed and encouraged their adult sons and daughters to immediately enlist in the INA.

The patriotism and sacrificial attitude of the Indian labour communities living in old Malaya and Burma cannot be underestimated. Inspite of being semi-aliens in theses lands, the parents of these youth took a big risk in encouraging their youth to enlist in the INA purely on patrtic grounds. There was no monetary benefit in joining the INA since it was a free service national army. The only tangible benefit was that these youth could avoid being used as forced labour by the occupying Japanese army who were expanding their infrastructure in south-east Asia to counter the British presence. Also during the war time, food was scarce to find, hence the recruits to the INA were assured of adequate food and other rations being supplied to them during the war operations. Of course, the biggest risk of being killed in action was always there and for this both the youth and their parents had to be commended for taking this ultimate risk.

Except for some officers of North-Indian lineage, most of the soldiers and sepoys from the rank and file of the INA were south Indians, particularly of Tamil descent. Many of the recruits were from the Madurai region of the old Madras Residency of the British Raj. These recruits were inspired by the speeches of the leader of their Thevar community Shri Muthu Ramalinga Thevar (popularly called MRT iyya), who time and against extolled the youth to leave for Burma to enlist in Netaji Bose's INA. There was certainly an excellent bond existing between Netaji Bose and MRT. All the movements of Netaji Bose were given direct information to MRT in Inida and he was on the surveillance of first the British intellegince before independence and later by the Intelligence Bureau from Delhi after independence. MRT was convinced that the freedom movement under Gandhi ji was doomed to failure because he felt the British were too deeply entrenched in India to go away due to a non-violent struggle from the local Indians. MRT was convinced that Netaji Bose was the only solution for getting rid of the Britishers from India using self-defence as the key to armed resistance. MRT was deeply inspired and motivated by the speeches and world activities of Netaji Bose and felt India's future lay in his hands.

Shri Muthu Ramalinga Thevar was instrumental in diverting much needed manpower and material for the INA in both Malaya and Burma. His excellent contacts among the Tamil community of South-East Asia, helped secure much needed moral and material support from the local Tamils there. While the dominant community in Burma were the Chettiars, who were traders and bankers by profession ,there were other communities that were more than willing to help the INA. Even after the purpoted death of Netaji Bose in Taiwan, MRT continued to maintain that Bose was very much alive and he had communication lines open to him. While the whole country was in grief on Netaji's death, MRT alone was non-chalant, happy in his thoughts that his national leader was very much alive in some corner of the world. This infuriated Nehru so much that after taking over as the interim PM of India, he detailed the Intelligence Bureau to keep tabs on MRT round the clock, hoping to glean some information on the whereabouts of Bose, in the event he was still alive.

There is no doubt that MRT was really a gem of a personality who also happened to be a mass leader among his native caste, the dominant Thevar Community of southern Tamil Nadu. It is also true that he maintained his name and fame among his people as a fair and generous man. He was a chronic bachelor till his very end and earned the reputation of being morally clean. During his later years he even supported the former ,legendary chief minister of old Tamil Nadu, Shri Kamaraj, to stand for his first election in the early 1950s. Even though Kamaraj belonged to the rival Nadaar Community, MRT pitched in to financially support Kamaraj for his election campaign. That Kamaraj won his election and later went on to become a legendary and charismatic CM of Tamil Nadu is now recorded history. It is extremely ironic that CM Kamaraj had to imprison his one time sponsor MRT due to caste riots that broke out in the southern districts following clashes between the dominant Thevar community and the down-trodden Dalit community. The most tragic part of this whole episode was that MRT actually died in prison following this long incarceration. This was certainly a dark chapter in the annals of the post-freedom movement.

There is still speculation how a gentleman like MRT could be accused as a casteist leader even though he was the chief supporter of Netaji Bose, a national leader who always believed in a society free of religion, caste and language barriers. How could MRT be accused of being part of a caste riot when he was such an ardent admirer and follower of Netaji Bose, whose national secularism was legion. Even today MRT's admirers talk of a strong campaign to besmirch the name of their leader who was against any caste conflagration. That matters got out of hand and both the warring communities had to stand trial in court is now history. But what happened next was something any patritotic Indian would be ashamed of. In the ensuing legal battle, the court requested any single witness to testify against MRT, since everybody either respected him or feared his mass influenze among his people. Only one single Dalit man was willing to testify against MRT as an eye witness to send him to jail. After his testimony in court, the witness was hacked to pieces by an enraged Thevar mob, who took revenge for the conviction of their bellowed leader MRT.

It was with great reluctance that CM Kamarajar allowed MRT to be sent to jail, just to maintain the law and order situation in the southern districts of Tamil Nadu. There is a strong theory that PM Nehru also had a hand in the eventual imprisonment of MRT under violent protests. Nehru was afraid that MRT was giving far too much publicity for Netaji Bose even after the latter was declared dead in the purpoted air crash in Taiwan. MRT often publicly declared that he continued to maintain secret contact with Netaji whom he claimed was in exile somewhere in remote central Asia. MRT had been openly declaring that it was only a matter of time before Netaji Bose would return to India and stake his claim to the PM chair, which many felt had been usurped by Nehru using the influenze of Gandhi ji, once the British left India. Nehru was deeply disturbed by his own intelligence reports that Bose was in fact alive and living in Soviet Russia. The alternate reason could be that Nehru, being part of the conspiracy to keep Bose interred in the Siberian prison under dictator Jospeh Stalin, was deeply worried that MRT would get at this hidden truth using his contacts abroad and would cause an insurrection to dethrone him from the PM chair. All in all, it is possible that Nehru pressurized CM Kamarajar to put MRT in jail at the earliest, to prevent him from collecting information on the actual whereabouts of Bose.

Even during his incarceration in prison, MRT continued to claim he was in touch with Bose. It is indeed unfortunate that MRT actually died in prison, putting a blackmark on the otherwise clean governance of CM Kamarajar. The decision to convict MRT on the grounds of creating communal tension is indeed controversial, given that MRT had a personal record of maintaining inter-caste amity even though he belonged to the dominant upper caste Thevar community, whose writ ran in the southern districts of Tamil Nadu. The decision to send MRT to prison must have rankled CM Kamarajar, since he was an early beificiary of MRT's largesse even though he belonged to the rival Naadaar caste. Today there are elders who still think that CM Kamarajar erred in turning against MRT, even thoug he could have upturned the decision using his massive influenze as the CM and also being close to the Central Government under PM Nehru. These elders from both the Thevar and other communities feel that there was a political vendetta attached to the legal action taken against MRT. They accuse Kamarajar of being a traitor and a back-stabber in the entire sordid drama of imprisoning MRT. The otherwise clean and corruption-free government of CM karamarar still hangs under the cloud vis-à-vis L"affaire MRT. History will certainly remember this unnecessary back-mark earned by the otherwise legendary administration of Shri Kamarajar.

One of the foremost and higher ranking officer of the INA will always be Commander Loganathan. Having served in the land operations of the INA with distinction in both the Malayan and Burma theatres of war, Cdr Loganathan was posted as the head of the local Governement-in-exile of the Andaman and Nicobar Islands soon after they were liberated by the Japanese Navy during the fag end of December, 1943. Cdr Loganathan was part of the flag hoisting ceremony at Port Blair, where the British Union Jack was brought down and the Indian tricolor was taken up. He accompanied Netaji Bose on his famous tour of the Andaman Islands, especially the memorable instant when Bose threw open the gates of the dreaded Cellular Prison, infamously known locally as Kaala Paani central jail. This symbolic act of Bose was a signal to the British Raj in Delhi that their days were indeed numbered. It was a brazen act of defiance to prove that no longer could the British keep Indian political prisoners in the Andaman Islands and torture them to death. Cdr Loganathn continued as the Lieutenant Governor of the Indian Government-in-exile at the Andaman Islands keeping the flag of free India flying till the final surrender of the INA in August 1945.

## 21. Netaji Bose - Father of Sacrifice

While Netaji Bose has been given various glorifying names, there is one thing that stood out in him a mile away the spirit of sacrifice. His burning patriotism for India made him take many daring decisions, including sacrificial ones. For example, when Gandhi ji expressed his displeasure in the victory of Netaji Bose for his second consecutive term as the president of the Indian National Congress, Bose had no hesitation in quitting the Congress, instead of picking up an argument with Gandhi. When Netaji Bose finished his one year ICS training stint, he quit his plum post just because he did not want to work with the British. That move of his will always be remembered for his absolute denial to the luxury of a rich life in power. Bose did not enter into any quarrel with Nehru, who was openly jealous of him and the mass appeal that Bose commanded with the public at large. There is no doubt that if Bose had chosen to take a confrontationist pose against even Gandhi, the winner would certainly have been Bose, based soley on the mass popularity he commanded. Bose would certainly have dented the image of Nehru, in the event a public spat between the two became inevitable. Even though Gandhi was considered the unifying mass leader of India, Bose's popularity had its own standing, which was awesome.

Bose took the narrow path of quitting the country to form an alliance with the natural enemies of the British Germany and Japan. Bose could very well have taken a confrontationist pose against the ahimsa of Gandhi, but his innate respect for his senior leader prevented him from hitting below the belt. The sacrificial spirit of first quitting the plum ICS post and then later resigning as the President of the Indian National Congress after being re-elected unanimously continued. His charisma was so deep that even when Gandhi fielded Mr. Seetharamiah as his personal choice for the INC Presidentship, Bose won the elections hands down. Instead of accepting the verdict of the electorate, Gandhi actually turned petulant and claimed openly that the defeat of Seetharamiah was a personal blow for him. This prompted Bose to resign without much ado.

The same spirit of sacrifice and endurance was shown by Bose when he volunteered to travel all alone with his junior compatriot of the INA, Capt. Abid Hassan, in a dark German submarine for close to 2500 kms underwater from Germany to Indonesia. The dangers of travelling in a submarine under the sea for long periods in those days was extremely dangerous given that submarines were a fairly recent invention. Not only that, Bose kept his cool and composure under very trying conditions during that long voyage of three months that straddled 3 continents and 2 large oceans. Netaji's spirit of sacrifice and his ability to withstand mental and physical hardships was recorded by the captains of the German and Japanese submarines that carried him from Europe to Africa and then onto Asia. The German skipper was full of praise for the calm and composure maintained by Bose and Capt. Hassan, who weathered the rolling and pitching of the submarine in the rough ocean currents. He had mentioned in his memoirs that Bose appreared just the kind of leader India needed to attain independence from the British.

It is also a matter of deep consternation to many how readily the foreign contemporaries of Bose took a liking for him. It was simply unbelievable how effortlessly Bose integrated with the psyche of all his known German and Japanese military officers and soldiers. There was a magnetism about him that fascinated his colleagues and friends around him. According to his colleague and senior INe fA officer Col. Shah Nawaz Khan, Netaji Bose was a person whom he found irresistable as a leader of men. There was an aura of directness and candidness one could not but love about Netaji Bose. He was mesmeric simply because there was never any airs around him. He treated all men and women with respect and never expected anyone to do more than his capacity for the INA. His sacrificial spirit was so legion that many were amazed at how much punishment Bose was taking on himself, both mental and physical stress combined. It was well known to the men of the INA that Bose had very little sleep during the nights, preferring to spend the early hours of the day on map-reading or strategic planning for the next day.

Netaji Bose had this endearing habit of giving away his food rations to the officers and soldiers under him. As head of the Indian Government in exile, he was entitled to special food rations from the Japanese high command. But rather than being selfish, he used to widely circulate his rations among his staff and soldiers, who used to have a shortfall very often. Netaji's vision of a free India was unmatched for its clarity of purpose. When one of his Muslim

INA officers, by the name of Lt.Nazeer lay badly wounded in a field hospital in Burma, Bose stayed overnight at the hospital inspite of grave risk of British aerial bombardment. Such was his devotion to the soldiers and officers of the INA, whom he considered as his own children. Netaji Bose was truly a peoples officer with excellent relations with all around him. People who have termed him a dictator have no idea at all about the excellent relations he maintained with the entire rank and file of the INA.

When Netaji Bose considered the option of escaping from India in 1941, he had a choice to exit India via Burma but realized that being a British controlled territory, he would face more problems. Moreover the route to Burma would be through the non-Hindi speaking belt of North-East India, which would be difficult to negotiate for him. Hence he decided to take the much longer route to Afghanistan through the hostile north-west frontier province. What Bose did was in effect take a Leap of Faith, given that the distance from his native Calcutta to Peshawar would be more than 2000 kms by road. The extreme sacrifice he was willing to undergo on this dangerous mission where he would be in disguise most of the time was truly enormous. Yet he was more than willing to take this extremely life-threatening journey just so as to go to Europe and meet up with Adolf Hitler and Benito Mussolini, simply keeping the freedom of India as his only mission. There was no prior appointment to meet either of these two foreign leaders and there were British secret agents all over the place in Kabul which was his first foreign stop after crossing British held Indian territory into Afghanistan. These agents had orders to capture Bose dead or alive anywhere in the world.

Afghanistan in those days was the happy hunting ground for secret agents of many countries including Russia, Britain and Italy. No foreigner was safe there as the Pathans of Afghanistan were considered very tough customers to deal with. Yet Bose felt much safer there than in British occupied India. The Pathans actually hated the British and it's a matter of pure history that the only country that Britain was never able to control in south Asia was Afghanistan. The Pathans were doughty fighters who could hold on to their territory for dear life, regardless of the consequences. Moreover the craggy mountains of the Hindu Kush Ranges were the famous hideouts of the Pathans which the British could never penetrate even after innumerable attempts. Bose took the bold decision of crossing over to Afghanistan only after considering all these geo-political equations.

After a difficult entry for an appointment with the Italian embassy in Kabul, they asked him to wait for some more days before arranging a dummy Italian passport for him in an Italian name. Those waiting days were a very dangerous time for Bose since many British and American secret agents were on the lookout for him. There was a bounty on his head, which had been announced recently. Inspite of all these problems Bose continued to hang out in dangerous Afghanistan, keeping the freedom of India as his chief focus. By nature, the local Afghani Pathans had a good opinion of Indians as they found them to be far more peace loving than the cunning British army. Hence some of the locals, even though they had reason to be suspicious of a strange Indian amongst them, did not blow the whistle on Bose, knowing that this would directly help the British cause. Afghanistan was a proud nation, that simply could not be subjugated by the British army for many decades. The Pathans were fierce fighters and no one could enter their hideouts in the Hindu kush mountains without their express permission. The all conquering British army had to taste bitter defeat many times as they tried to break through the rock like defence of the Afghanis in their rocky mountains.

Even the trip to Russia in a Japanese aircraft in mid-August 1945 was a Leap of Faith across all sides. Here was the leader of a Government-In-Exile going to a foreign land without any direct invitation ,during the throes of the second world war. Here was the leader of an exiled Army trying to take refuge in a country who was directly aligned against his sponsoring country. Bose was taking a wild chance of entering a nation that had been at war with his closest ally, Germany. There was every chance of his asylum request being rejected outright and even the outside chance of him being taken prisoner by the Russians. Bose was in effect trying to pally up to dictator Joseph Stalin of Russia, who had been back-stabbed by dictator Adolf Hitler of Germany by his invasion of Russia a few years ago. The situation was extremely volatile, but Bose decided his decision was the best since he always had a soft corner for Russia and her socialist doctrines. His sentiment to the communist system of governance threw his caution to the winds and little did he know what fate had in store for him, when he entered Russian territory in Siberia through the Manchurian border. Bose was taken into Siberia in a Russian military jeep which entered Manchuria, at that time under Japanese occupation. That was the last time the civilized world ever saw Netaji Bose again. Bose was never seen again till his purported death in a freezing Siberian prison in the mid-1950s.

# Index

## A

Africa viii, 5, 13, 14, 15, 17, 18, 21, 33, 34, 42, 44, 49, 59, 72, 100
African 13, 14, 31, 34
Ambedkar 67, 76, 79
American x, 10, 14, 18, 21, 35, 36, 37, 42, 43, 44, 55, 56, 59, 60, 83, 85, 102
Andaman 28, 29, 31, 86, 87, 89, 96, 97
Arabian 9, 82
Arunachal x, xi, 36, 81
Asylum 59

## B

Bangalore 46
Bhaghat 68
Bombay 6, 68, 71, 73, 74
Brigade xiv, 92
Britain 6, 9, 17, 26, 27, 32, 34, 38, 56, 57, 60, 62, 63, 68, 74, 75, 101
British vii, viii, ix, xii, xiv, 3, 5, 6, 9, 10, 11, 13, 14, 15, 18, 19, 21, 22, 23, 26, 27, 28, 29, 30, 31, 33, 34, 35, 36, 37, 38, 41, 42, 44, 45, 46, 47, 49, 50, 51, 52, 53, 55, 56, 59, 60, 62, 63, 64, 67, 68, 69, 70, 71, 72, 73, 74, 75, 76, 77, 80, 83, 85, 86, 88, 89, 91, 93, 94, 95, 96, 97, 99, 100, 101, 102
Buddha 21, 80, 85
Burmese ix, 36, 37, 38, 39, 41, 51, 53

## C

Cadets x, 2
Calcutta viii, 9, 27, 31, 36, 68, 71, 74, 87, 89, 101
Castro 42, 43, 44
Chennai x, xi, xii, xiii, xiv, xv, 22, 31
Churchill 26, 62
Coimbatore ix, x
Congress ix, xi, xii, xiii, xiv, 1, 3, 5, 6, 7, 23, 27, 42, 63, 64, 67, 68, 69, 71, 72, 75, 76, 77, 78, 79, 82, 83, 84, 86, 87, 89, 90, 99

## D

Dairen 61
Desert 13
Dimapur 46, 50
Dysentery 26

## E

Eastwards 9
Europe viii, 5, 10, 11, 13, 14, 15, 17, 32, 33, 34, 46, 49, 55, 59, 62, 68, 72, 75, 77, 85, 86, 100, 101

## F

Fighter xiv
France 25, 30, 87
Freedom xiv, 5, 75
Frontier 9, 36

## G

Gandhi vii, viii, ix, xi, xii, xiii, 1, 2, 3, 5, 6, 9, 15, 23, 27, 33, 34, 42, 43, 45, 46, 47, 49, 63, 67, 68, 69, 70, 72, 74, 75, 76, 77, 78, 79, 80, 82, 84, 85, 86, 87, 88, 89, 90, 91, 94, 95, 99
German ix, 5, 10, 13, 14, 15, 17, 18, 19, 33, 34, 46, 86, 87, 100
Governor 29, 31, 49, 74, 97
Guerilla 35, 36, 37, 38, 42, 43, 73

## H

Hassan 17, 18, 19, 100
Himalayas x, xi, 9, 36, 81, 82
Hindus 30, 38, 71, 72, 75, 76, 77, 80
Hindustan 77, 80
Hindutva 76
Hiroshima x, 55, 56
Historians 6, 7, 10, 55
Hitler 5, 9, 10, 13, 14, 15, 17, 19, 34, 45, 59, 61, 62, 86, 87, 101, 102
Hockey x
Hunger 78

## I

Imphal 36, 37, 43, 44, 45, 46, 47, 51, 53
Indian ix, x, xi, xiii, 1, 2, 3, 5, 6, 10, 11, 13, 14, 15, 18, 19, 21, 22, 23, 25, 26, 28, 29, 31, 33, 34, 35, 36, 37, 38, 41, 42, 43, 45, 46, 50, 51, 53, 56, 65, 67, 68, 69, 70, 71, 72, 73, 74, 75, 77, 78, 79, 81, 82, 83, 84, 87, 88, 90, 91, 93, 95, 96, 97, 99, 100, 101, 102
Indira vii, xiii, 2, 82, 84, 85, 88, 90
Island 29, 73
Italian 9, 10, 19, 33, 34, 102

## J

Japanese ix, 2, 5, 10, 11, 14, 18, 19, 21, 22, 23, 26, 28, 29, 31, 33, 34, 35, 36, 37, 38, 41, 45, 46, 49, 50, 51, 53, 55, 56, 59, 60, 61, 63, 83, 84, 85, 86, 88, 89, 93, 96, 100, 102
Jhansi xiii, xiv, 23, 35, 51, 52, 74
Jinnah 6, 76, 77, 78, 79, 80
Joseph 1, 60, 61, 62, 102
Jungle 23

## K

Kamaraj 94, 95
Kamarajar 95, 96

Karachi 6, 71, 73, 82
Kashmir 2, 44, 73, 82
Kerala 93
Khyber 44
Kohima 36, 37, 43, 44, 47, 49, 50, 51
Krishnan 74

## L

Ladhakh 81
Lankan 35
Legion 13, 14
Loganathan 31, 96

## M

Madras ix, xi, xiii, xiv, xv, 2, 22, 25, 28, 31, 68, 71, 93, 94
Madurai viii, xii, xiii, xv, 25, 87, 89, 93
Malaria 26, 52
Malaya vii, x, xiii, 2, 25, 26, 27, 36, 42, 43, 53, 56, 73, 87, 88, 93, 94
Manchuria 59, 60, 63, 83, 102
Mandalay 36, 37, 38, 86
Manipur xii, xiii, 41, 44, 46, 88, 91
Marina xi
Marshal 13, 14, 34
Mexico 42, 43, 59
Military x, 2, 13, 41, 45
Moirang 41, 44, 51
Moscow 10, 19, 60, 61
Mukherjee 84
Muslim 6, 9, 30, 53, 71, 72, 76, 77, 78, 79, 80, 91, 100
Mussolini 9, 10, 101
Mutiny 6, 53, 69, 71, 74

## N

Nazeer 52, 53, 101
Netaji i, iii, vii, viii, ix, x, xi, xii, xiii, xv, xvi, 1, 2, 3, 5, 6, 7, 9, 10, 14, 19, 21, 22, 23, 25, 26, 27, 29, 30, 31, 33, 35, 36,

# Index

37, 38, 41, 42, 44, 50, 51, 52, 53, 56, 59, 60, 61, 63, 64, 65, 67, 68, 69, 72, 74, 76, 77, 79, 83, 84, 85, 86, 87, 88, 89, 90, 91, 92, 94, 95, 96, 99, 100, 101, 102
Nicobar  29, 96
Northern  17, 19, 36, 37, 46

## P

Pakistan  2, 30, 71, 73, 76, 77, 79, 80, 81, 82
Partition  75
Pathans  19, 44, 101, 102
Peshawar  9, 101
Pradesh  x, xi, 36, 81, 93
President  xiv, xvi, 25, 55, 64, 99
Province  9
Publisher  iv
Punjab  80

## R

Radiation  56
Ramalinga  25, 89, 94
Regiment  xiii, xiv, 23, 35, 51, 52
Renkoji  viii, 65, 84, 85
Rivers  80
Rommel  13, 14, 34
Russia  9, 23, 27, 31, 56, 57, 59, 60, 61, 62, 63, 64, 81, 86, 87, 95, 101, 102
Russian  1, 10, 56, 59, 61, 62, 64, 65, 88, 102

## S

Samadhi  vii
Siberia  1, 60, 102
Singapore  xiii, 21, 22, 23, 25, 27, 31, 33, 41, 42, 51, 53, 56, 60, 86, 88, 93

Soviet  10, 19, 59, 60, 61, 62, 64, 83, 84, 95
Stalin  xi, xii, 1, 59, 60, 61, 62, 63, 64, 96, 102
Stilwell  37
Subash  ix, x, 1, 3, 10, 17, 22, 27, 41, 42, 43, 44, 68, 74, 85
Submarine  17
Surrender  55

## T

Taiwan  viii, 37, 59, 61, 64, 65, 83, 84, 88, 94, 95
Thevar  xii, xiii, 87, 89, 94, 95, 96
Tibetan  81
Troops  13

## U

U-boat  17, 18

## V

Vajpayee  vii, xiv, xvi, 84, 85
Vietnam  35, 42, 43, 44, 88
Volunteers  27
Voyage  17

## W

Werner  17, 18

## Y

Yunnan  36, 37

www.ingramcontent.com/pod-product-compliance
Ingram Content Group UK Ltd.
Pitfield, Milton Keynes, MK11 3LW, UK
UKHW022154230426
12049UKWH00003BA/86